What Every Woman Should Know Before Joining the Marine Corps

A.J. Cabrera

Copyright © 2013

All rights reserved. No part of this book may be reproduced in any form or by any electronic or mechanical means including information storage and retrieval systems- except in the case of brief quotations in articles or reviews - without the permission in writing from its publisher, A.J. Cabrera. This book is a work of the author's experience and opinion. Names, characters, places and incidents are either the product of the author's imagination or are used fictitiously. Any resemblance to actual persons, living or dead, or to actual events or locales is entirely coincidental.

All brand names and product names used in this book are registered trademarks, registered trademarks, or trade names of their respective holders. I am not associated with any product or vendor in this book.

Although the author and publisher have made every effort to ensure that the information in this book was correct at press time, the author and publisher do not assume and hereby disclaim any liability to any party for any loss, damage, or disruption caused by errors or omissions, whether such errors or omissions result from negligence, accident, or any other cause.

This book is not intended as a substitute for the medical advice of physicians or financial professionals. The reader should regularly consult a physician in matters relating to his/her health and particularly with respect to any symptoms that may require diagnosis or medical attention. The author and publisher are in no way liable for any misuse of the material. Published by A.J. Cabrera.

Table of Contents

Section 1: What You Need To Know BEFORE You Join

Don't Just Listen To Your Recruiter, Do the Research

Grasp What Becoming A Marine Really Means

Don't Gain Weight- Ever!

Get A Thick Skin

If You Pull the Female Card, Don't Expect to Get Respect

It's A Man's Marine Corps (or so they like to think)

Sexual Responsibility

You Are Still A Lady

The Things You Do While "Off Duty" Will Affect You

You ARE Going to Break A Nail

It Is Not Really Four Years

You Will Be Watched (and Judged) Wherever You Go

You Are Trained to Fight and Possibly Die, Not Travel

Marriage

Section 2: What Your Parents Need to Know

Becoming A Marine Parent

Parent Do's and Don'ts

Letters From Recruits

Mail and Packages

Protecting Your Recruit's Privacy

Section 3: What You Need to Know About the Marine Corps

History of the Marine Corps

Birthplace of the Marine Corps

History of Marine Corps Recruit Training

Marine Corps Motto & Slogans

Marine Corps Hymn

Marine Corps Mission

Marine Corps Boot Camp Terminology

Core Values: Honor, Courage, Commitment

Structure of Training Battalions and Platoons

Drill Instructor Creed

Recruiters

Uniforms

Ranks in the Marine Corps

Marine Corps Structure

Marine Corps Birthday Ball

Women in the Marines

Corps Respect

Section 4: What You Will Go Through in Boot Camp

Recruit Training

Yellow Footprints

Drill Instructors

Practical Application & Written Test

MRP: Medical Rehabilitation Platoon

MCMAP & Pugil Sticks

Marine Week

Initial Drill Evaluation

Classroom Training

Haircuts & Hygiene

Every Marine is A Rifleman

Four Rifle Range Safety Rules

Grass Week & Shooting Positions

Firing Week & Qualification Day

Confidence and "O" Courses

Health and Wellness During Boot Camp

Combat Water Survival

Combat Conditioning

The Crucible

Section 5: Graduation

Preparing for Graduation

Group Visits

Lodging

Professional Photos and Videos

Family Orientation, Family Day and Graduation

Motivational Run

Press Release Template

Section 6: What Happens After Boot Camp

Recruiter's Assistance

10-Day Leave

PDS: Permanent Duty Station

Glossary

Resources

References

Author Bio

More Books by A.J. Cabrera

Thank You

Section 1: What You Need To Know BEFORE You Join

Don't just listen to your recruiter, do the research

Recruiters must meet a monthly quota. The very first thing you need to know is that recruiters must meet a quota every month. This means they have to talk to a lot of potential candidates in order to get two to enlist each month. Now, I'm not saying they will do anything unethical, but in some cases if they can promise you certain things to get you to sign on the dotted line, some recruiters may do it. This doesn't mean that all recruiters are like this. In fact, they are taught not to do these sort of things. Unfortunately, like everything else in life there are always a few spoiled apples in the bunch.

Make sure that you protect yourself by being well informed and researching your options. Do not rely solely on what the recruiter is telling you. Make sure that you do the research and that you know that what you are signing up for. If you have a friend or relative that has gone through the Marine Corps and has more experience, invite them to sit down and talk with the recruiter. Then get their opinion to see if it sounds like the recruiter you are dealing with is telling you the truth. Even though it may have been awhile since they served, they can still offer some good advice to help you.

If it isn't in writing, then it simply doesn't exist. It doesn't matter what a recruiter tells you, it only matters if you have it in writing. It can be pretty devastating to go through boot camp and MCT and then get orders to a school that wasn't what you thought you picked. It happens all the time, however. It is your responsibility to make sure that what is in writing reflects what you and your recruiter agreed upon. If something seems incomplete or "off", you need to have it corrected. Do not allow anyone to intimidate you or explain away the error. Do not sign anything you do not agree with.

Verify everything your recruiter is telling you. Recruiters cannot guarantee that you will be assigned to a particular state like Hawaii, or guarantee that you will spend the next four years of active duty not being deployed overseas. You can be guaranteed an opportunity to go into the MOS of your choice as long as your ASVAB scores are eligible for that career.   However, if you fail that school, the Marine Corps will assign you to a job in accordance with its needs. So make sure that everything recruiter is telling you is true and backed up by your own research.

Don't let your recruiter talk you into something you don't want to do. Make sure you take the time to research the different jobs the recruiter is trying to get you to sign up for. Regardless of the way he describes the jobs, you want to make sure that this is something that you will be interested in doing.   If your recruiter is trying to push you into a particular job that you aren't particularly interested in, it could be that it is easier to get that spot or that there are more vacancies than maybe the MOS that you are interested in.   Be sure to stand your ground. This is your life and your career. Take the time to do the research so that you know the next four years will be spent doing something you enjoy.

Grasp what becoming a Marine really means

What are the "right" reasons to join?
Obviously by now you know that the Marine Corps has a reputation for being the toughest branch in the military. In fact, this is probably one of the reasons you are considering joining the Marine Corps. However, it is extremely important to look beyond the reputation and ask yourself why you want to join the Marine Corps specifically. Why not the Air Force or the Army? Everyone has their reasons, what are yours? If you want to look good in a uniform,

or be able to brag to everyone around you that you are a Marine, then may want to keep moving. As a Marine you will be able to do these things, but they are not a good enough reasons to join. Being a Marine means that you are committing to upholding high moral and ethical standards and ideals for the rest of your life. The title Marine is one that you will never lose. Once you earn it, it is yours for life. This should be treated as an honor, not a right. It should not be abused or carried around haphazardly. As a Marine you will be trained to fight your enemies. Make no mistake about it, this is not a travel or college program, this is an indoctrination into a group of warriors. You are expected to perform as a warrior first, not a college student.

What will you be giving up/leaving behind?

Another factor that is important to consider is what you will be leaving behind when you enlist in the Marine Corps. Will you be able to leave your friends and family and everything you know? Yes, you will be able to visit them but you will be stationed most likely far away from them. Make sure that you understand that your first duty will be expected to be to the Marine Corps. While the Marine Corps supports family units, that truth is that they expect 110% of your loyalty and time first. The needs of the Marine Corps are expected to be put in top priority in your life, fitting in friends and family when you can. If you are a parent, this means that you will have to fill out a family care plan that assigns your custody rights over to a person that you trust with your child. This is an extremely important issue to consider. You must make sure that the person you assign this responsibility to would not take advantage of the situation.

Ask yourself what you expect to get out of joining and then see if it matches up to the needs of the Marine Corps. What do you think you expect to get from joining the Marine Corps? Where do you think it will lead you? What do you feel you have to offer? These are all very important questions to ask yourself. Take the time to answer them. It is equally important to research what the needs of the Marine Corps are and determine if you can meet some of these needs. Would you be a valuable asset to the needs of the Marine Corps or would you be a hindrance? Being honest with yourself and confronting these questions now could save you a lot of time and frustration down the road. If you think you can handle living a lifestyle of high ethical integrity and character then Marine Corps may be a good choice for you. However, if you have habits or addictions that could be in contrast to the needs of Marine Corps, you need to honestly assess whether you think your service would be a help or hindrance. Admiration from civilians is great but if you don't think you can hack it, then it is best that you not join.

It's A Man's Marine Corps (or so they like to think)

Men outnumber women approximately 100 to 1.
You will, without a doubt, be working in an

environment with almost all males. It is no surprise that males outnumber women in the military. In the Marine Corps this is especially true. You will be surrounded by males who will know before you arrive at your first duty station that you are coming. The Marine Corps is not only a predominately male environment, it is also a small environment. Therefore, how you conduct yourself professionally and around these males is crucial to your reputation. If you fail to respect yourself and others, you will get a reputation for that and it will follow you throughout your Marine Corps career.

Men can be a distraction to your mission. Resist the urge to get caught up in dating male colleagues. At least for the first year. Focus on your career in the Marine Corps and not on dating other male Marines. If you choose to date Marines, be sure to assume that anything that happens between the two of you will be talked about amongst other male Marines. Assume that this will be the case and conduct yourself accordingly. There have been cases (too many to count) of female Marines who have trusted their relationships only to have been betrayed. Then, when the break up happens, they suddenly receive a less than desirable reputation. Keep your goals clear about what you want to do in the Marine Corps and why you came in. If you choose to date other male Marines, especially those you work with, make sure that you are professional and respectable at all times.

Chauvinism/ Sexism. Unfortunately, in every working environment there are still issues dealing with sexism and chauvinism. The Marine Corps is no different. However, the Marine Corps has done a lot in proactively preventing this kind of treatment. What happens in the day-to-day, real-life workings may contain an element of chauvinism and/or sexism. Usually it starts out by joking back and forth as a way to build camaraderie. Eventually, it escalates into full blown disrespect. Treat other people how you want them to treat you. Therefore, if you are okay with dealing out disrespectful jokes or attacks at others under the guise of "kidding around," then expect the same thing will happen to you. The Marine Corps does not corner the market on this. It can happen at any job. Therefore, it is important to remain professional with your colleagues. If you go out for drinks after work or you consider them friends, have respect for yourself and for others by avoiding any kind of chauvinism or sexist comments disguised as jokes. This simply protects yourself and others from unprofessional conduct that can get out of hand quickly.

Your effort will determine the respect you receive. If you start out your Marine Corps career by respecting yourself and others, presenting a professional character that lets others know that you will not be disrespected, then you will have a better time receiving the respect you deserve. You teach people how to treat you. Therefore, if you do the work alongside your other Marines you will be known as someone who can be dependable and counted on. However, if you slack off or find excuses as to why you cannot participate, you will receive that reputation as well. When you are talking about a career that involves fighting alongside others in a war, you do not want a reputation as someone who cannot be counted on to have others backs when it counts.

Sexual Responsibility

Cautionary tales after getting out of boot camp and into the fleet. Before you leave boot camp your drill instructors will talk with you about avoiding the pitfalls of getting out there and getting married and/or pregnant. They will tell you that one third of you will be either married or pregnant (or both) within the year. It is true, so believe it. You will likely be in the best shape of your life. You will probably have lost weight and want to take your new body out for a spin. Avoid the urge to hook up during this time. Your entire career could be delayed if you get pregnant. You want to at least make it through all of your training and get out into the fleet before considering a relationship. If you do end up pregnant, you could be delayed in your training.

Pregnancy and STD's. It goes without saying that you must practice safe sex in all situations. The military can be a breeding ground for sexually transmitted diseases. It used to be that you would actually get into real documented trouble if you were diagnosed with a STD. I don't know if this is still the case but I do know that you are now property of the government and they can penalize you for "damaging" their property. Oh, and make no mistake, they DO own you. When you are in boot camp they perform every kind of medical physical that you could possibly hope for. They also give you the most comprehensive sexual education classes you have ever seen. I was very impressed by the responsibility they take to educate recruits about sex. It makes sense considering the statistic I mentioned above.

I remember sitting in the medical office with several other female recruits. A male and female nurse were telling us about the importance of safe sex. Then the male pulls out a purple condom, unrolls it and proceeds to stretch the entire thing over his fist all the way up to his elbow while telling us that if any guy says that it "doesn't fit" not to trust or believe him. So yeah, there's really no excuse not to use protection.

What happens if you do become pregnant? In the "old" days if you became pregnant in the Marine Corps, you had the option of getting out. The reason I why was in large part due to the fact that many women would join in search for a husband. Now they don't give you that option. If you become pregnant you will be put on light duty and accommodated around your pregnancy, but you will be expected to continue training as you can. If you have completed all of your training and have been deployed to your permanent duty station then you will be working a job that is conducive to your condition.

If you believe that you cannot be deployed after your baby is born, think again. There are parents who have been deployed upon returning from maternity leave. It can happen so this is something to keep in mind. That is why you must have a family care plan set in place. Family is great but the Marine Corps still requires that you give them 110% over everything else. This is something to seriously think about.

You are still a lady

The Marine Corps isn't going to try to change your sex. Many females make the connection that in order to be "tough" in the Marine Corps they must adapt male habits such as smoking, drinking, chewing tobacco, cursing, etc. There is nothing more unbecoming. Represent yourself as a woman warrior by maintaining your own personality. Males do not look upon females who adopt these habits with any more respect than another female. Respect by male Marines come from your character and integrity and pulling your own weight. The Marine Corps does not expect you to become a male. In fact, in boot camp you will be taught by drill instructors to represent yourself as a lady, a woman Marine. This doesn't mean you have to be a damsel in distress, nobody is going to have time for that either. It means that you do not make excuses for your sex. You draw on your strengths as a woman and use them toward the benefit of serving the Marine Corps.

Represent the Corps as a lady. This includes conducting yourself with professionalism and etiquette. You will get more respect by conveying that you are a mature and reliable woman Marine who knows who she is and can serve with honor alongside other Marines. Do not fall into the trap of joking around with male Marines to the point that they think they can take advantage of harassing remarks. This can quickly go downhill. Then you will be put in the position of sounding like someone who cries foul when they suddenly decide they don't like how they are being treated after participating in the back and forth harassing banter. Keep your expectations of others for how they should treat you clear from the start. Treat others with respect the way you expect them to treat you. Stay consistent in your actions.

Perception of others. Perception is reality. This can be unfortunate at times. As a woman Marine you are set to a higher standard whether you like it or not. As a woman Marine, you will be judged and looked at more closely. If you screw up, it is going to be remembered longer. If you do well, you will also be remembered. Either way, you will be judged in everything you do. Help yourself out by making sure that your reputation is spotless.

I was stationed at my MOS school when one of my male Marine friends tell me they heard a rumor that another Marine (a friend I thought) was going around telling other male Marines that he had slept with me. This was pretty careless and stupid of this young Marine, considering I outranked him and was in a leadership billet that he fell under. He was very immature and thought he was going to gain "stud" points with the other male Marines.

So how did I handle it?

I brought all the male Marines together who had confirmed that they heard this from this Marine's own mouth and brought them to this Marine. Then, in front of all of his buddies I asked him if he had in fact said this about me. I reminded him about the commitment he made to uphold the Marine Corps values of honor, courage and commitment before he answered.

He confessed and told everyone that he lied about the rumor. He was incredibly embarrassed, which he should have been. He then apologized and we all moved forward.

The point is, never be afraid to stand up for your reputation and confront those who, in their immaturity, would seek to damage it. Like it or not, there is a double standard among men and women. You do NOT want a reputation in the Marine Corps as a female who sleeps around. It is almost impossible to get rid of this reputation once it has circulated.

The things you do "off duty" will affect you

You are never really off duty. I cannot stress

enough the importance for women in the Marine Corps to maintain a stellar reputation. It is one hundred times harder to gain the same respect as a female warrior than it is a male. There have been too many females who have given women Marines a bad name that often the expectation from male Marines is that all women Marines sleep around. Your actions change that perception or enforce it.

Do not believe for one second that what you do off duty stays out of the Marine Corps family. You are stationed on a base in a small community. You make friends with other Marines. Your environment is entirely surrounded by Marines almost constantly. Do not embarrass yourself by doing things that will disgrace yourself or your fellow Marines. For example, getting drunk is never an excuse for your actions. Lose your mind over the weekend and expect that when you report to work Monday morning, everyone will be talking about it. Nicknames are born in this kind of environment and viciously stick throughout your Marine Corps career.

Reputation is everything as a female Marine. If you want to be taken seriously by your colleagues then you need to respect yourself enough to take yourself seriously. This is a conscious decision that all women Marines must make. You will be the result of a long lineage of women Marines who have fought for the right to serve and make advances in the Marine Corps. Do not disgrace our history by acting like a silly, easy female. Make sure your self-esteem is high by getting into college and taking advantage of Marine Corps activities like sports. Get involved in helping others. Do what it takes to make your self-worth validated by things that do not include constantly flirting with male Marines.

This section is probably one of the most important things you should know before joining the Marine Corps. It will dictate your experiences in the Marine Corps and whether those experiences will be pleasant or a living hell.

You WILL break a nail

Don't bother joining if you don't expect to get dirty. The Marine Corps can be a dirty job (but somebody's got to do it). Please do not think that just because you are a female that you will not be expected to carry you own weight. You are going to get plenty dirty. In fact, that is the expectation in the Marine Corps. Even if you work in an office as part of your MOS, you will still have PT and MCMAP (martial arts) training that will take you outside. Add to that daily police calls (this is where you pick up trash around your building), gas chamber and rifle range requalification and more.

You will be expected to do the same dirty jobs as the males. There is no room to play the damsel in distress in the Marine Corps. Marines are trained to fight and to do what it takes to win battles and come home alive. You are expected to perform the same duties as male Marines when the time is called for it. Trying to get out of these duties shows poor teamwork and character. It will get you the reputation for not being dependable. That may not seem like a big deal when you are in the fleet, but when you are talking about being deployed in a war zone it is literally the difference between life and death. No one is going to carry your weight for you. If you do not perform, you will be written up and can in some cases have legal action taken against you.

You have to expect some bumps and bruises.
If you haven't figured out by now the Marine

Corps is a physical occupation. You must stay in the best shape that you can and expect that through your training you will collect your fair amount of bumps and bruises. Whining and crying about every little injury is not going to get you sympathy. It's going to get you a reputation that you can't handle your fair share of the work load. This is not to say that you should "suck it up" and not report any injuries. To neglect doing that would be ridiculous. Your body is a valuable asset to the Marine Corps and to your survival. You must take care of your body and report injuries that could get worse if not treated. When it comes to superficial bruising and minor scratches, don't be whiny about every single one.

It's not really four years

Your enlistment is four years active, four years reserve for a total of 8 years. If you decide to sign up for active duty, you will be signing up for four active duty years. Additionally, you will also be signing up for four inactive duty years. This means that when you leave the Marine Corps at the end of serving your four years, you can be recalled for four more years after that time. Do not let the recruiter tell you anything different. Make sure you know how long you are signing up for. There are some MOS careers that will require you to sign up for five years active duty so make sure that you know the terms of the enlistment before you sign up for that career.

You can be recalled during your reserve status. As I said before, you can be recalled any time after your active duty status has elapsed within your four year reserve status. In war time, this can be very common. Also, realize that if you sign up to be a reservist, contrary to what you may be told, reservists are activated FIRST. So thinking that you are just going to go to boot camp, your MOS training and then go back to your life without a worry is naïve.

Stop Loss. In a time of war, the government can issue a "stop loss." This means that all service members who are supposed to EAS (End of Active Service), or get out of the Marine Corps, will be kept in for as long as the stop loss has been ordered. This could be for any period of time, even over a year. Understand that this is a possibility in today's world and that if you enlist you could face this issue depending on the needs of the Marine Corps.

You will be judged (and watched) everywhere you go

Do not trust anyone with your reputation. Do not assume that anyone will be watching out for your reputation. It doesn't matter what they say to you or how much they promise that those "pictures/video" will not be shown to anybody. Do NOT compromise your reputation for anyone or anything. As a Marine you will be admired and watched everywhere you go. As a female Marine, you will be scrutinized for everything you do or don't do that is expected of a Marine. It may be unfair but it is reality.

You cannot change other people or their perceptions. The only thing you can do is ensure that the way you carry yourself is in accordance with the honor and traditions of the Marine Corps.

Understand that what you do now will follow you to different duty stations. Had a wild night, went out drinking and did some things you regret the morning after? Report to your job only to find out that EVERYBODY knows about it. That's pretty much how it works. When you leave one duty station to report to another, your reputation follows you. You will have people from your old duty station call ahead to your new one to give them the 4-1-1 on who is coming their way. If it involves a less than respectable reputation, you can be sure that the gossip is already circulating.

They know who you are before you get there. This is why they know who you are before you get there. They have had a head's up warning. Your reputation will dictate what kind of greeting you get. If you have screwed up in the past, the only thing you can do is to try to create a new reputation by staying consistent and dependable. Slowly, people's perceptions MAY change. It is better to stay respectable from the beginning instead of having to do damage control that may or may not ever go away. On the other hand, you may hear about people that you are about to meet from your friends who may have served with them in the past. If this is the case, then do what you would want to have done to you and give new people you meet the benefit of the doubt. Allow them to build their fresh start with you and take them as you see them. At least you will not be a party to any kind of personal discrimination against them before really getting to know them.

You are trained to fight and possibly die, not travel or go to college

The days of joining for the benefits are over. In the past, people would join the military who had no real direction with what to do with their life. The military offered a place to live, a steady paycheck, a chance to travel and go to college. In fact, it used to be that criminals who came in front of a judge were given the choice to either enlist in the military or go to jail.

Times have changed, however. The military has become more selective in who it allows to enlist. Government cut backs have also played a role in how many new service members can join each fiscal year. All those who apply will not be accepted for various reasons. The two most common reasons are medical injuries and/or criminal offenses.

The military still offers college and other benefits for service. The point is to consider joining for reasons that go deeper than for just the benefits. I wouldn't advise any person to join the military solely for the benefits. In this day and age with so many conflicts going on around the world, it is unwise and naïve not to believe that you may find yourself in the middle of a combat zone instead of a classroom.

Understanding the meaning of becoming a Marine is important to avoid disappointment. It is crucial to understand the importance for why you want to join the Marine Corps. It is important to join for the right reasons and not for just college and/or traveling. The expectation of believing that all you will have to do is travel and go to college will disappoint you when you figure out what the realities of military life are. Serving as a Marine can be a very challenging and rewarding, yet difficult job. In some cases, the experience can make or break you. Do not delude yourself into thinking that it is all glamorous or that you will be constantly admired by others.

It is a life of service, not privilege. To join the Marine Corps means that you understand you are joining a life of service, not privilege. That means you have agreed to fight for your country and pay the ultimate sacrifice, if necessary. It means that you have an obligation to defend and protect the U.S. Constitution and the civilians of this country. This is a huge responsibility and great honor that should not ever be taken lightly.

Marriage

Do not fall victim to the traps of getting married too young or too soon. Unfortunately, this is such a common occurrence in the military, especially within the first year that young Marines graduate boot camp. Hormones being what they are, it is tempting to get carried away and think that you will live happily ever after. Most of the time this is not the case. It adds unneeded pressure on your new career and can create new problems. It is wise to wait at least a year after you have been assigned to your permanent duty station to assess whether or not you are ready to make such a commitment. The Marine Corps does not care that you are a newlywed and want to be stationed with your new husband. They will try, but it is always the needs of the Marine Corps that come first.

Do not marry for the BAH housing, rules have changed. There have been incidents where new Marines think it is a good idea to get married in order to get Base Allowance Housing (BAH). BAH is extra money the military gives you every month to supplement off base housing expenses. Some new Marines have even persuaded a friend to get married on paper even though they are not a couple. This is not only fraud it is idiotic. Please do not try this. The extra allowance isn't that much more to warrant going through all that trouble.

Think about how this will affect your career. Remember that the Marine Corps foundation is based on core values that Marines are expected to uphold at all times. Honor, courage and commitment are not just words. They are an ideal that each Marine is expected to strive to live every day. Lying to obtain more money is just plain wrong. Marrying too young or too early can be detrimental to your military career if not thought out completely.

Section 2: What Parents Need To Know

Becoming A Marine Corps Parent

Dear Parents,

Welcome to one of the most unique families in the world. By proxy, you will be inducted into a group that is older than our Constitution. It is an honorable organization with a long history of warriors. You are about to be the parent of one of those warriors. Without the knowledge and facts of what to expect, this journey can be scary. It is important to learn myth from fact and to ensure that you do everything you can do to support your future Marine and keep yourself from worrying.

If you are a Marine veteran, or come from a Marine Corps family already, this book is a great resource. It can help you compare your experiences with how the Marine Corps is conducting its training now. Many things have changed throughout the history of boot camp, but many things have not. This book can provide you with an opportunity to brush up on what's new and discuss what is the same. This guide has information from multiple official United States Marine Corps web sites and endeavors to be as current as possible.

The 13 weeks of recruit training will fly by before you know it. While you won't be there personally to witness the transformation, you will be able to learn what is happening to your recruit. The best thing you can do is educate yourself on what your recruit is going through so that you can learn what will be expected of him/her as a United States Marine. This book is designed to help you do just that. It will give you a glimpse of what it is like as a recruit in boot camp and what you, as a parent, will need to know. It will also explain how you can help your recruit while he/she is in boot camp and what not to do. When graduation rolls around, you will be prepared to see your new Marine and understand exactly how the graduation process works.

Also, we will explore what happens to your Marine after boot camp. His/her journey is only beginning at that point. There is still much more that your Marine will learn as he/she is sent to Marine Combat Training, his/her Military

Occupational Specialty (MOS) school and then into the fleet. The adventure doesn't stop with graduating boot camp. Your Marine is going to need your support for a long time. The best thing you can do is prepare yourself with the education and knowledge that you can be a successful Marine parent.

This is an exciting time for your future Marine. He/she is embarking on a journey that few will ever understand or comprehend. It will change their lives in so many ways. It is important as their parent that you understand why they call the Marines, "The Few. The Proud." It is a way of life that is difficult to explain unless you have lived through it. However, this book is going to do its best to explain it in a way that makes you beyond proud that your son or daughter chose the Marine Corps as a foundation for the way to live an honorable life of service to our country.

Parent Do's and Don'ts

1. Make it Christmas for them Everyday (or as much as possible)
How do you do this? You write letters. A TON of letters. Recruits often feel homesick. Especially in the beginning as it is swirling around in their minds that they may have made a huge mistake. Boot camp is kind of traumatic (hello, understatement of the year). The best way to help them through it is to keep communication open with them. Recruits eagerly look forward to receiving letters. They feel very disappointed when they do not receive any. Let them know that it is okay if they do not have time to write (because often they do not). DO NOT send care packages. They will go

straight to the trash. If there is ANYTHING in a care package that a drill instructor can pick apart to humiliate the recruit then they WILL! Keep it to letters.

Make sure your letters stay upbeat. Do not burden the recruit with things they have no control over. They need to stay emotionally focused on their training. Keep the letters drama free and instead focus on the positive things going on back home. Do not draw on the outside of the envelopes. This could attract some unwanted attention from a drill instructor and that's the LAST thing your recruit needs or wants.

A tip for keeping ahead of the letter writing is to write them on a computer and print them out. Keep a ready supply of stamps on hand. Use specialty paper with pictures on it if you want to give it a variety and make it fun. Send a couple of photos from back home if you want to but make sure it uplifts the recruit's mindset and keeps his/her focus on the training.

2. It is "recruit", NOT "Marine" (Not Yet)

Do not address your recruit as a "Marine." That honor is reserved for when the recruit graduates and receives his/her eagle, globe and anchor. Until then, he/she is simply addressed as "recruit."

3. DO NOT Miss Graduation.

Do whatever it takes to plan ahead so that you can be there to witness one of the best days of your child's life. Being a Marine is something that he/she will always be from graduation on. You do not want to miss such the commemoration of such a life-altering event. Bring a couple of cameras, and all the batteries and supplies you can carry. Be prepared to walk- a lot. Wear comfortable shoes and clothing and dress appropriately depending on the weather.

If you have to miss graduation, let your recruit know that you want him/her to purchase the graduation video (VHS/DVD).

DO NOT walk across the parade deck at graduation. This is a sacred area and is reserved for those who have earned the title "Marine." It is out of respect that you stay off of it. Regardless of the circumstances, do not do it.

First Phone Call

When recruits arrive on the Recruit Depot, they

will make a phone call home. They do not have much time to talk, however, and will not be able to chat or answer any questions. They are given a script to repeat that basically tells you that they have arrived safely and that they will contact your in three to five days by postcard with their mailing address. Sneak in an "I love you" if you can, but know that they are lined up next to other recruits making the same phone call and drill instructors directly behind them. They won't be able to say much more than what they are told to say. It will happen quickly, so take comfort in knowing that you received the phone call and they have arrived safely.

Also, these phone calls occur in the middle of the night. There is a reason why they coordinate the arrival of recruits on the Depot in the middle of the night. It is to disorient them while introducing them to a new world. Expect your phone call to come late at night. Adopt the theory that "no news is good news." If you are not receiving any calls from them then most likely they are safe and training is progressing for them just fine.

Letters From Recruits

Do not expect very many letters from your recruit. Although recruits are given time to write, they also have many other responsibilities. Many will need to use this time to catch up on work and study. Understand this and the pressure they are under. Do not get onto them in your letters or put pressure on them to write. Keep sending your letters out and just know they appreciate receiving them. It is normal for many recruits to write home expressing distress. They may tell you that they feel they have made a mistake and want to go home. Continue to be supportive and encouraging of their decision to join the Marine Corps. Tell them how proud you are of them and their decision. This whole experience is new and a huge culture shock from what they are used to. As they progress in training, they will ease out of this feeling.

When your recruit is able to write, he/she will confide in you all of his/her emotions and experiences. It would be wise not to share these thoughts on a public message board. Your recruit needs to share these experiences without fear of them being made public. These feelings may only be temporary and could change in a few days or a week. Keep your recruit's letters private. Drill instructors read the message boards and WILL bring up anything that could embarrass your recruit. Keep this in mind. It's hard enough to get through boot camp without becoming a target by a drill instructor. Drill instructors are known to give little nicknames based on a recruit's habits or screw-ups. Please do not contribute to making it easier for the drill instructors. Be the safe place that your recruit can confide in you about all the experiences he/she is going through.

Mail and Packages at Marine Corps Boot Camp

The very first letter you'll receive from your recruit will be a form letter. You're going to get it about 10 to 14 days after they leave. In the letter will be the recruit's mailing address. This address will remain the same for the boot for the recruits entire time in boot camp. If for some reason you do not receive a form letter, contact your recruiter. The recruiter should be able to get you the address. In some cases, recruits can request that mailing addresses not be given out even a family members. Recruiter's must honor this request. This bears repeating, but do not send any care packages to your recruit. Address your letters to your recruit as follows: Rct Last name, First name

Do not put any other rank other than Rct which means recruit. You should also refer to them as recruit when you address the envelope. Failing to do this can cause unnecessary attention from the drill instructors. Also, do not put your recruit's social security number on the envelope. There are two instances where you would use an alternative mailing address. The first is if your recruit is assigned to PCP (Physical Conditioning Platoon). The mailing address in this case will be the PCP until the recruit is assigned to a regular platoon. The second instance would be if your recruit is sent to MRP (Medical Rehabilitation Platoon). If your recruit becomes an injured or killed this is where he/she would go.

Mail Delivery
Mail is delivered at the Depot in (MCRD) Monday through Saturday. There could be a few days delay depending on the training schedule to getting the mail into you recruit's hand. Your recruit's mail will never be held for disciplinary reasons, however.

Protecting Privacy
The Internet is a breeding ground for identity

theft and other dangers. Therefore it is critical to protect your recruit's privacy as much as possible. This includes the following:

Be very mindful of what you share with others online. You should never share any personal information with anyone in chat rooms or other web sites. Even though some of these web sites are Marine Corps oriented, they're not secure.

Under no circumstances should you give your recruit's last name, e-mail address, phone number, birthdate and addresses. Do not give out your recruit's graduation day either. Clever criminals can take this information and use it to their benefit.

Do not share anything online at your recruit wants to remain private. This is the recruit's journey, and as such he/she needs to know that the details of his/her experiences are kept private.

Keep conversations with others limited too generic topics. No matter how comfortable you feel was someone online, do not drop your guard.

If there is anything that you wish to share be sure to get your recruit's permission first.

Section 3: What You Need to Know About the Marine Corps

Brief History of the United States Marine Corps

On November 10, 1775, the Second Continental Congress meeting in Philadelphia passed a resolution stating that "two Battalions of Marines be raised" for service as landing forces with the fleet. This resolution established the Continental Marines and marked the birth date of the United States Marine Corps. Serving on land and at sea, these first Marines distinguished themselves in a number of important operations, including their first amphibious raid into the Bahamas in March 1776, under the command of Captain (later Major) Samuel Nicholas. The first commissioned officer in the Continental Marines, Nicholas remained the senior Marine officer throughout the American Revolution and is considered to be the first Marine Commandant. The Treaty of Paris in April 1783 brought an end to the Revolutionary War and as the last of the Navy's ships were sold, the Continental Navy and Marines went out of existence.

Following the Revolutionary War and the formal re-establishment of the Marine Corps on 11 July 1798, Marines saw action in the quasi-war with France, landed in Santo Domingo, and took part in many operations against the Barbary pirates along the "Shores of Tripoli". Marines took part in numerous naval operations during the War of 1812, as well as participating in the defense of Washington at Bladensburg, Maryland, and fought alongside Andrew Jackson in the defeat of the British at New Orleans. The decades following the War of 1812 saw the Marines protecting American interests around the world, in the Caribbean, at the Falkland Islands, Sumatra and off the coast of West Africa, and also close to home in operations against the Seminole Indians in Florida.

During the Mexican War (1846-1848), Marines seized enemy seaports on both the Gulf and Pacific coasts. A battalion of Marines joined General Winfield Scott's army at Pueblo and fought all the way to the "Halls of Montezuma," Mexico City. Marines also served ashore and afloat in the Civil War (1861-1865). Although most service was with the Navy, a battalion fought at Bull Run and other units saw action with the blockading squadrons and at Cape Hatteras, New Orleans, Charleston, and Fort Fisher. The last third of the 19th century saw Marines making numerous landings throughout the world, especially in the Orient and in the Caribbean area. Following the Spanish-American War (1898), in which Marines performed with valor in Cuba, Puerto Rico, Guam, and the Philippines, the Corps entered an era of expansion and professional development. It saw active service in the Philippine Insurrection (1899-1902), the Boxer Rebellion in China (1900). and in numerous other nations, including Nicaragua, Panama, Cuba, Mexico, and Haiti.

In World War I the Marine Corps distinguished itself on the battlefields of France as the 4th Marine Brigade earned the title of "Devil Dogs" for heroic action during 1918 at Belleau Wood, Soissons, St. Michiel, Blanc Mont, and in the final Meuse-Argonne offensive. Marine aviation, which dates from 1912, also played a part in the war effort, as Marine pilots flew day bomber missions over France and Belgium. More than 30,000 Marines served in France and more than a third were killed or wounded in six months of intense fighting.

During the two decades before World War II, the Marine Corps began to develop in earnest the doctrine, equipment, and organization needed for amphibious warfare. The success of this effort was proven first on Guadalcanal, then on Bougainville, Tarawa, New Britain, Kwajalein, Eniwetok, Saipan, Guam, Tinian, Peleliu, Iwo Jima, and Okinawa. By the end of the war in 1945, the Marine Corps had grown to include six divisions, five air wings, and supporting troops. Its strength in World War II peaked at 485,113. The war cost the Marines nearly 87,000 dead and wounded, and 82 Marines had earned the Medal of Honor. While Marine units took part in the post-war occupation of Japan and North China, studies were undertaken at Quantico, Virginia, which concentrated on attaining a "vertical envelopment" capability for the Corps through the use of helicopters. Landing at Inchon, Korea in September 1950, Marines proved that the doctrine of amphibious assault was still viable and necessary. After the recapture of Seoul, the Marines advanced to the Chosin Reservoir only to see the Chinese Communists enter the war. After years of offensives, counter-offensives, seemingly endless trench warfare, and occupation duty, the last Marine ground troops were withdrawn in March 1955. More than 25,000 Marines were killed or wounded during the Korean War.

In July 1958, a brigade-size force landed in Lebanon to restore order. During the Cuban Missile Crisis in October 1962, a large amphibious force was marshaled but not landed. In April 1965, a brigade of Marines landed in the Dominican Republic to protect Americans and evacuate those who wished to leave. The landing of the 9th Marine Expeditionary Brigade at Da Nang in 1965 marked the beginning of large-scale Marine involvement in Vietnam. By summer 1968, after the enemy's Tet Offensive, Marine Corps strength in Vietnam rose to a peak of approximately 85,000. The Marine withdrawal began in 1969 as the South Vietnamese began to assume a larger role in the fighting; the last Marine ground forces were out of Vietnam by June 1971.

The Vietnam War, longest in the history of the Marine Corps, exacted a high cost as well with over 13,000 Marines killed and more than 88,000 wounded. In the spring of 1975, Marines evacuated embassy staffs, American citizens, and refugees in Phnom Penh, Cambodia, and Saigon, Republic of Vietnam. In May, Marines played an integral role in the rescue of the crew of the SS Mayaguez captured off the coast of Cambodia. The mid-1970s saw the Marine Corps assume an increasingly significant role in defending NATO's northern flank as amphibious units of the 2d Marine Division participated in exercises throughout northern Europe. The Marine Corps also played a key role in the development of the Rapid Deployment Force, a multi-service organization created to insure a flexible, timely military response around the world when needed. The Maritime Prepositioning Ships (MPS) concept was developed to enhance this capability by pre-staging equipment needed for combat in the vicinity of the designated area of operations, and reduce response time as Marines travel by air to link up with MPS assets.

The 1980s brought an increasing number of terrorist attacks on U.S. embassies around the world. Marine Security Guards, under the direction of the State Department, continued to serve with distinction in the face of this challenge. In August 1982, Marine units landed at Beirut, Lebanon, as part of the multi-national peace-keeping force. For the next 19 months these units faced the hazards of their mission with courage and professionalism. In October 1983, Marines took part in the highly successful, short-notice intervention in Grenada. As the decade of the 1980s came to a close, Marines were summoned to respond to instability in Central America. Operation Just Cause was launched in Panama in December

1989 to protect American lives and restore the democratic process in that nation.

Less than a year later, in August 1990, the Iraqi invasion of Kuwait set in motion events that would lead to the largest movement of Marine Corps forces since World War II. Between August 1990 and January 1991, some 24 infantry battalions, 40 squadrons, and more than 92,000 Marines deployed to the Persian Gulf as part of Operation Desert Shield. Operation Desert Storm was launched 16 January 1991, the day the air campaign began. The main attack came overland beginning 24 February when the 1st and 2d Marine Divisions breached the Iraqi defense lines and stormed into occupied Kuwait. By the morning of February 28, 100 hours after the ground war began, almost the entire Iraqi Army in the Kuwaiti theater of operations had been encircled, with 4,000 tanks destroyed and 42 divisions destroyed or rendered ineffective. Overshadowed by the events in the Persian Gulf during 1990-91, were a number of other significant Marine deployments demonstrating the Corps' flexible and rapid response. Included among these were non-combatant evacuation operations in Liberia and Somalia and humanitarian lifesaving operations in Bangladesh, the Philippines, and northern Iraq. In December 1992, Marines landed in Somalia marking the beginning of a two-year humanitarian relief operation in that famine-stricken and strife-torn nation. In another part of the world, Marine Corps aircraft supported Operation Deny Flight in the no-fly zone over Bosnia-Herzegovina. During April 1994, Marines once again demonstrated their ability to protect American citizens in remote parts of the world when a Marine task force evacuated U.S. citizens from Rwanda in response to civil unrest in that country.

Closer to home, Marines went ashore in September 1994 in Haiti as part of the U.S. force participating in the restoration of democracy in that country. During this same period Marines were actively engaged in providing assistance to the Nation's counter-drug effort, assisting in battling wild fires in the western United States, and aiding in flood and hurricane relief operations. The Marine Corps continued its tradition of innovation to meet the challenges of a new century. The Marine Corps Warfighting Laboratory was created in 1995 to evaluate change, assess the impact of new technologies on warfighting, and expedite the introduction of new capabilities into the operating forces of the Marine Corps. Exercises such as "Hunter Warrior," and "Urban Warrior" were designed to explore future tactical concepts, and to examine facets of military operations in urban environments.

During the late 1990's, Marine Corps units deployed to several African nations, including Liberia, the Central African Republic, Zaire, and Eritrea, in order to provide security and assist in the evacuation of American citizens during periods of political and civil instability in those nations. Humanitarian and disaster relief operations were also conducted by Marines during 1998 in Kenya, and in the Central American nations of Honduras, Nicaragua, El Salvador, and Guatemala. In 1999, Marine units deployed to Kosovo in support of Operation

Allied Force. Soon after the September 2001 terrorist attacks on New York City and Washington, D.C., Marine units deployed to the Arabian Sea and in November set up a forward operating base in southern Afghanistan as part of Operation Enduring Freedom.

In 2002, the Marine Corps continued to play a key role in the Global War on Terrorism. Marines operated in diverse locations, from Afghanistan, to the Arabian Gulf, to the Horn of Africa and the Philippines. Early 2003 saw the largest deployment of Marine forces since the Persian Gulf War of 1990-91 when 76,000 Marines deployed to the Central Command area for combat operations against Iraq. The I Marine Expeditionary Force, including Task Force Tarawa and the United Kingdom's 1st Armored Division, were the first conventional ground units to enter Iraq in late March as part of Operation Iraqi Freedom. Fixed-wing and helicopter aircraft from the 3d Marine Air Wing provided continuous close air and assault support to Marine and coalition units as they drove deeper into Iraq. On the ground, Marines from I MEF moved nearly 400 miles from the Kuwait border to Baghdad and Tikrit, Iraq, and eliminated the last organized resistance by Iraqi military forces. Although I MEF would transition to stabilization and security operations and then redeploy to the U.S. by late September, I MEF began preparing for a return to Iraq in early 2004.

The adaptability and reliability of Marine forces continued to be highlighted around the world from the Horn of Africa to Haiti and to the Philippines.

Across the U.S., Marine units from both coasts fought and contained wildfires, and also supported hurricane relief efforts in various parts of the country. In December, 2004, a tsunami struck numerous nations in the Indian Ocean region killing more than 150,000 and causing enormous devastation. Marine units from III MEF were immediately deployed to Thailand, Indonesia, and Sri Lanka to assist in disaster relief operations. In early 2005, the II Marine Expeditionary Force replaced I MEF in Iraq as the primary focus began to shift to partnership operations with the Iraqi Security Forces. Marine units continued to provide air and ground support to Operation Enduring Freedom in Afghanistan. Closer to home, the flexibility and responsiveness of the Navy/Marine team was exhibited during

September and October when nearly 3000 Marines and sailors conducted search and rescue, humanitarian relief, and disaster recovery operations in Louisiana and Mississippi in the aftermath of hurricanes Katrina and Rita.

Today's Marine Corps stands ready to continue in the proud tradition of those who so valiantly fought and died at Belleau Wood, Iwo Jima, the Chosin Reservoir, and Khe Sanh. Combining a long and proud heritage of faithful service to the nation, with the resolve to face tomorrow's challenges will continue to keep the Marine Corps the "best of the best."

Tun Tavern: Birthplace of the Marine Corps

During the American Revolution, many important political discussions took place in the inns and taverns of Philadelphia, including the founding of the Marine Corps. A committee of the Continental Congress met at Tun Tavern to draft a resolution calling for two battalions of Marines able to fight for independence at sea and on shore. The resolution was approved on November 10, 1775, officially forming the Continental Marines. As the first order of business, Samuel Nicholas became Commandant of the newly formed Marines. Tun Tavern's owner and popular patriot, Robert Mullan, became his first captain and recruiter.

They began gathering support and were ready for action by early 1776. Each year, the Marine Corps marks November 10th, The Marine Corps Birthday, with a celebration of the brave spirit which compelled these men and thousands since to defend our country as United States Marines.

History of Marine Corps Recruit Training

For most of the Marine Corps' history, there was no highly structured program of instruction for Marine recruits, such as we know today. Only in the last 90 years have there been centralized recruit depots with the mission of transforming civilians into basically trained Marines prepared to perform on the battlefield. Early Marine recruit training was conducted at various posts and stations by noncommissioned officers who trained recruits in the "principles of military movements" and the use of the rifle. Commandant Franklin Wharton, who led the Corps from 1804 until his death in 1818, was the first to recognize the need for organized training and created a school for Marine recruits at the Marine Barracks in Washington where young men learned the basics of discipline, drill, the manual of arms and marksmanship.

 The sea-going nature of the Marine Corps, however, coupled with the recurring shortages of money and men, kept the Marine Corps system for training recruits quite primitive throughout the 19th century. In 1911, however, Major General William P. Biddle, 11th Commandant of the Marine Corps, instituted some sweeping changes that would have profound and long-lasting effects on the training of Marines.

On assuming command of the Corps, Biddle made two months of recruit training mandatory and set up four recruit training depots – at Philadelphia, Norfolk (later at Port Royal, South Carolina), Puget Sound, Washington, and Mare Island, California. Mare Island became the sole west coast depot during the following year, and east coast recruit training was shifted to Parris Island, South Carolina, in 1915. The training program Biddle outlined included drill, physical exercise, personal combat, and intensive marksmanship qualification with the recently-adopted M1903 Springfield rifle.

General Biddle's innovation met its first real test during World War I when the Corps expanded from about 15,000 to nearly 70,000

Marines in less than 18 months. During that period, the recruit training load expanded from 835 to a peak of 13,286. Living conditions at both depots were Spartan and the training was intense. Upon completion of recruit training, Marines received additional pre-embarkation training at Quantico, Virginia, and still more training after arriving in France.

During the summer of 1923, the west coast recruit depot was moved from Mare Island to San Diego, California. Training programs at the two recruit depots included three weeks of basic indoctrination, an equal period of time on the rifle range, and the final two weeks was occupied in bayonet drill, guard duty, drill and ceremonies.

During September 1939, shortly after the German invasion of Poland, expansion of the

Corps from 18,000 to 25,000 Marines was authorized. The recruit syllabus was halved to four weeks to meet this goal, but the result was a decline in training standards and rifle qualification rates plummeting to new lows. From this experience came the realization that seven to eight weeks is the minimum amount of time required for adequate recruit training. The World War II recruit training formula did not vary greatly from World War I except in the overwhelming number of Marines to be trained --- nearly half a million men over a four year period. It was during the war, though, that a third recruit training facility was established at Montford Point, North Carolina, to train some 20,000 black Marines. Recruit training was fully integrated and Montford Point put to other use in 1949.

The outbreak of war in Korea saw recruit training spring into high gear once again as fresh replacements, only weeks beyond recruit training, performed creditable combat service at the demanding battles of Inchon, Seoul, and the Chosin Reservoir. After the war, the recruit syllabus returned to 10 weeks from the war-shortened 8-week schedule.

The period of active American involvement in Vietnam, from 1965 through 1970, saw recruit training reduced to nine weeks. Graduates moved directly from their depots to either Camp Lejeune or Camp Pendleton for additional infantry training, much as their World War II counterparts had done.

The past forty years have witnessed the continuing close scrutiny of the Marine Corps recruit training program. Concerted efforts have been made to eliminate the excesses that had crept into the system over the years while at the same time retaining those elements of the recruit training experience that have produced a highly trained and motivated fighting force. Officer supervision and special training units, along with other innovations for enhancing the effectiveness of recruiting training, were implemented during these decades. The goal, as articulated by Commandant of the Marine Corps General Randolph McCall Pate in 1956, has been "to preserve, protect, and improve the actual system of recruit training which has served us so well."

Marine Corps Motto & Slogans
"Semper Fi"

The Marine Corps adopted the motto "Semper Fidelis" in 1883. Prior to that date three mottoes, all traditional rather than official, were used. The first of these, antedating the War of 1812, was "Fortitudine." The Latin phrase for "with courage," it was emblazoned on the brass shako plates worn by Marines during the Federal period. The second motto was "By Sea and by Land," taken from the British Royal Marines "Per Mare, Per Terram." Until 1848, the third motto was "To the shores of Tripoli." Inscribed on the Marine Corps colors, this commemorated Presley O'Bannon's capture of the city of Derna in 1805. In 1848, this was revised to "From the halls of the Montezumas to the shores of Tripoli."

"Semper Fidelis" signifies the dedication that individual Marines have to "Corps and country," and to their fellow Marines. It is a way of life. Said one former Marine, "It is not negotiable. It is not relative, but absolute...Marines pride themselves on their mission and steadfast dedication to accomplish it."

"The Blood Stripe"

Marine Corps tradition maintains that the red stripe worn on the trousers of officers and noncommissioned officers, commonly known as the "blood stripe," commemorates those Marines killed storming the castle of Chapultepec in 1847. Although this belief is firmly embedded in the traditions of the Corps, it has no basis in fact. The use of stripes clearly predates the Mexican War.

In 1834, uniform regulations were changed to comply with President Andrew Jackson's wishes that Marine uniforms return to the green and white worn during the Revolutionary War. The wearing of stripes on the trousers began in 1837, following the Army practice of wearing stripes the same color as uniform jacket facings. Colonel Commandant Archibald Henderson ordered those stripes to be buff white. Two years later, when President Jackson left office, Colonel Henderson returned the uniform to dark blue coats faced red. In keeping with earlier regulations, stripes became dark blue edged in red. In 1849, the stripes were changed to a solid red. Ten years later uniform regulations prescribed a scarlet cord inserted into the outer seams for noncommissioned officers and musicians and a scarlet welt for officers. Finally, in 1904, the simple scarlet stripe seen today was adopted.

"The Few. The Proud."

"The Few. The Proud. The Marines." is the Marine Corps' advertising slogan. It won a place on Madison Avenue's Advertising Walk of Fame during Advertising Week 2007. "This slogan reflects the unique character of the Marine Corps and underscores the high caliber of those who join and serve their country as Marines," said Maj. Gen. Richard T. Tryon, commanding general, Marine Corps Recruiting Command.

"Ooh Rah"

An expression of enthusiasm used by Marines in various situations. Specifics regarding the origin of the spirit cry are sketchy and we're still searching for accurate and reliable information.

"First to Fight"

Marines have been in the forefront of every American war since the founding of the Corps. They have carried out over 300 landings on foreign shores. They have served everywhere, from the poles to the tropics. Their record of readiness reflects pride, responsibility and challenge.

"Leathernecks"

In 1776, the Naval Committee of the Second Continental Congress prescribed new uniform regulations. Marine uniforms were to consist of green coats with buff white facings, buff breeches and black gaiters. Also mandated was a leather stock to be worn by officers and enlisted men alike. This leather collar served to protect the neck against cutlass slashes and to hold the head erect in proper military bearing. Sailors serving aboard ship with Marines came to call them "leathernecks."

Use of the leather stock was retained until after the Civil War when it was replaced by a strip of black glazed leather attached to the inside front of the dress uniform collar. The last vestiges of the leather stock can be seen in today's modern dress uniform, which features a stiff cloth tab behind the front of the collar. The term "leatherneck" transcended the actual use of the leather stock and became a common nickname for United States Marines.

"Devil Dogs"

In the Belleau Wood fighting in 1918, the Germans received a thorough indoctrination in the fighting ability of the Marines. Fighting through supposedly impenetrable woods and capturing supposedly untakeable terrain, the persistent attacks, delivered with unbelievable courage soon had the Germans calling Marines "Teufelhunde," referring to the fierce fighting dogs of legendary origin.

"Esprit de Corps"

The "spirit" of a unit. This spirit is commonly reflected by all members. It implies devotion and loyalty to the Marine Corps, with deep regard for history, traditions and honor.

"Uncommon Valor"

Refers to the victories in World War II, especially at Iwo Jima, the largest all-Marine battle in history. Admiral Nimitz's ringing epitome of Marine fighting on Iwo Jima was applied to the entire Marine Corps in World War II: "Uncommon valor was a common virtue."

"Gyrenes"

The term "gyrene" is a jocular reference to Marines which was first used in England as early as 1894. It was used in the United States around the time of World War I. Its exact origin is unknown, but it did appear to have a derogatory meaning in its early usage. It has been suggested that the term may embody a reference to pollywog, a naval slang term for a person who has not yet "crossed" (the equator), hence, a landlubber.

"Jarhead"

A slang term used by sailors as early as World War II to refer to members of the Marine Corps, drawing the term from the resemblance of the Marine dress blues uniform, with its high collar, to a Mason jar.

Source: The National Museum of the Marine Corps and Heritage Center.

Marine Corps Hymn

MARINE HYMN LYRICS

From the halls of Montezuma to the shores of Tripoli ,

We fight our country's battles in the air, on land and sea.

First to fight for right and freedom, and to keep our honor clean.

We are proud to claim the title of United States Marines.

Our flags unfurled to every breeze from dawn to setting sun.

We have fought in every clime and place where we could take a gun.

In the snow of far-off northern lands and in sunny tropic scenes.

You will find us always on the job the United States Marines.

Marine Corps Mission

Every Marine is a rifleman and combat ready, willing and able to stand shoulder-to-shoulder in battle. Every Marine also has a specific area of expertise that contributes to the total force and mission readiness. Every Marine is committed to the Core Values in service to the country.

Marine Corps Boot Camp Terminology

Marine Corps Motivational Sayings	
Semper Fi	Short for Semper Fidelis, Latin for "Always Faithful"
Ooh Rah!	Motivational statement in acknowledgement or agreement
Terms about the Depot	
MCRD	Marine Corps Recruit Depot, also called "The Depot"
PI	Parris Island (MCRD PI)
SD	San Diego (MCRD SD)
RTB	Recruit Training Battalion
Plt	Platoon

DI	Drill Instructor
SDI	Senior Drill Instructor
CO	Commanding Officer
CG	Commanding General
CMC	Commandant of the Marine Corps
MRP	Medical Rehabilitation Platoon
PCP	Physical Conditioning Platoon
Graduation Terms	
Parade Deck	Graduation: ceremonies take place on the parade deck. Do NOT walk across the parade deck.
Moto Run	Graduation: the last battalion run taken together

	on Thursday morning prior to family day
Theater	Graduation: classroom-style seating in a theater where families will hear information from the DIs
Viewing Stands	Graduation: the bleachers for families to sit on during ceremonies
Training Terminology	
IST	Initial Strength Test
PFT	Physical Fitness Test
PT	Physical Training
IT	Boot camp term, extra attention and extra PT
Quarter Deck	This is where you get IT'd

Ink stick	Pen
Lead stick	Pencil
Knowledge	School book/notebook
Guideon	Platoon flag
Titles of Recruit Training "Jobs"	
Guide	In charge of the entire platoon, carries the guideon
Squad Leader	In charge of the squad
Scribe	The recruit who keeps notes and records for the DI
House Mouse	Makes sure the cleaning supplies are put up and the "Duty Hut" is clean, usually more than one recruit
Orders, Acknowledging Orders	

As you were	Disregard my last statement
Aye, aye	A term used by a subordinate to a senior in acknowledgement of an order
Carry On	An order to resume previous activity after interruption
Marine Corps Gear	
Weapon	M16A2 (NEVER called a gun)
Canteen/water bowl	Water bottle
Moon Beam	Flashlight
Clothing/Personal Property	

Cover	Uniform headgear
Blouse	Any shirt that is part of the Marine Corps uniform
Trousers	Pants
Go Fasters	Running shoes
Skivies	Underwear
Portholes	Glasses (also referred to as BC glasses where the BC can stand for Boot Camp or Birth Control - Birth Control because they are so ugly there isn't a chance of...well, they're that ugly)
Verbs/Activities	
Chow	Meal time, also the food itself

Hydrate	Drinking water (a critical component of recruit training and being a Marine)
Hygiene	Shower (or any other way to clean yourself)
Drill	Marching
Swab	Mop
Mini Grinder	Little bit-o-hell (moving bunkbeds to one side so they can drill with weapons)
Space, Direction, Buildings	
Rack	Bed

Squad Bay	Where they sleep (also referred to as "the house" or barracks)
Duty hut	Office (Room in the Squad Bay where the DI staff has a desk, computer and a cot- the DIs are with our Recruits 24/7 they do not knock off at 5pm and get to go home)
Head	The bathroom
Whiskey Locker	Closet in the squad bay where cleaning supplies are kept
Foot Locker	Recruits store their gear in a footlocker at the foot of their "rack"

Overhead	Roof/ceiling
Bulkhead	A wall
Porthole	Window
Hatch	Door
Ladderwell	Stairs
Port	Left
Starboard	Right
Bow	Front
Aft	Back
Other Terms	
Suzie	Girl back home (girlfriend)
Jody	(Guy that the girl "is cheating on him with")
T-Day	Training day
H-day	Holy day
Fresh blood	Recruits

| **Doc** | FMF Corpsman (FMF = Fleet Marine Force) |

Core Values: Honor, Courage, Commitment

Recruits Demonstrate Core Values during Team Week

Recruits learn, from day 1, that to be a Marine is to do what is right in the face of overwhelming adversity. To understand how to do what is right they are taught about ethics and our core values. The Corps' core values are Honor, Courage and Commitment. These values make up the bedrock of a Marine's character. During recruit training, recruits are taught these core values and the numerous others attached to them, such as integrity, discipline, teamwork, duty and esprit de corps.

Team Week is a time for recruits to demonstrate that they understand how to do what is right, and that they are taking ownership of ethics and our core values.

Team Week tests team building efforts and allows recruits to work in an environment of minimal supervision. At this point in training, recruits are expected to demonstrate a higher degree of maturity and are able to assume more responsibility, and some recruits will work in small groups around the Depot and will not be under the direct supervision of their drill instructors. The recruits have developed a high degree of discipline and teamwork, and are now functioning as well drilled unit. Team Week is their first opportunity to show their drill instructors and company officers how close they are to becoming Marines.

The recruits are now over half-way through recruit training. While there is no official status of a senior recruit, at this phase of training the recruits are on the verge of entering Third Phase where they will face the challenges of Basic Warrior Training (BWT) and the Crucible.

Structure of Training Battalions and Platoons

There are two facilities for recruit training. They are called Marine Corps Recruit Depot (MCRD). They are located in San Diego, California and Parris Island, South Carolina. The acronyms for each are MCRD SD and MCRD PI.

Though there are some exceptions, for the most part, the Mississippi River is the dividing point for which MCRD your son or daughter will attend. Recruits west of the Mississippi River attend MCRD SD. Recruits east of the Mississippi River attend MCRD PI. All female recruits attend MCRD PI (no exceptions).

Each MCRD includes Recruit Training Battalions, or RTB. Each RTB has a color and crest associated with it. RTBs are divided into companies, and each company is divided further into platoons. Each platoon has a 4-digit number. Each company runs a 13-week training schedule and graduate on the same day. A battalion is identified by number, 1-4. Each company is identified by a letter in alphabetical order. The platoon is identified by a 4-digit number, with the first number indicating which battalion they are from. The following is the breakdown of each MCRD.

San Diego MCRD
1st Battalion (red)
(platoon numbers begin with 1xxx)
Alpha Company

Bravo Company

Charlie Company

Delta Company

2nd Battalion (yellow)

(platoon numbers begin with 2xxx)

Echo Company

Fox Company

Golf Company

Hotel Company

3rd Battalion (blue)

(platoon numbers begin with 3xxx)

India Company

Kilo Company

Lima Company

Mike Company

Parris Island MCRD

1st Battalion (red)

(platoon numbers begin with 1xxx)

Alpha Company

Bravo Company

Charlie Company

Delta Company

2nd Battalion (yellow)

(platoon numbers begin with 2xxx)

Echo Company

Fox Company

Golf Company

Hotel Company

3rd Battalion (blue)

(platoon numbers begin with 3xxx)

India Company

Kilo Company

Lima Company

Mike Company

Quebec Company

4th Battalion (maroon)

(platoon numbers begin with 4xxx)

November Company

Oscar Company

Papa Company

Drill Instructor Creed

Your recruit will be introduced to his/her drill instructors for the first time at the end of the first week after arriving in boot camp. Indeed, this is one of the defining moments of a recruit's training.

How do recruits move from first meeting their Drill Instructors to holding them in the highest esteem in just 13 weeks? The drill instructor creed, below, says it all. These are not just words; this is the 24-hours-a-day, 7-days-a-week, 13-week mindset of every instructor with your recruit. The drill instructors do not go home at the end of the day when they are training a platoon--they stay with the platoon. They sacrifice much to live by this creed and they will make sure your son or daughter earns the title of "United States Marine".

United States Marine Corps Drill Instructor Creed

"These recruits are entrusted to my care. I will train them to the best of my ability. I will develop them into smartly disciplined, physically fit, basically trained marines, thoroughly indoctrinated in love of the Corps and country. I will demand of them and demonstrate by my own example, the highest standards of personal conduct, morality and professional skill."

Dedication ~ Leadership ~ Integrity

The Recruiters

Every Marine, in every Military Occupational Specialty (MOS), plays a crucial role in the overall mission of the United States Marine Corps. Marine Corps Recruiters, MOS 8411, must be thoroughly familiar with the enlistment process from applicant prospecting to preparation for recruit training. Their duties include, but aren't limited to: screening applicants to determine eligibility relative to physical defects, moral character, criminal involvement, age, drug abuse, education, etc.; scheduling working applicants to take the Armed Services Vocational Aptitude Battery test at the MEPS; arranging for physical examinations of mentally qualified applicants;

and preparing all required enlistment documents.

As the parents and/or family of a Marine Corps applicant or recruit, you likely have many questions. You may or may not find your son or daughter's recruiter to be helpful in answering your questions. Bear in mind, your son or daughter's recruiter has a mission to accomplish and the recruiter's duties are to the Marine Corps and the applicants. Don't fret; there are plenty of other avenues through which you can find the answers you're looking for.

The following four websites are great resources for information on the Marine Corps:

www.Marines.mil

Official site for the United States Marine Corps.

www.Marines.com

Marine Corps culture, eligibility, history, roles in the corps, benefits of service and more.

www.RecruitParents.com

Includes information about recruit training (boot camp), schedules, terminology, expectations, and perhaps most importantly, venues to talk with other parents--novices just like you, as well as "expert" parents who've been down this road and experienced the same uncertainties and pride.

www.MarineParents.com

Provides education and support for Marine Corps families, provides "a Place to Connect & Share™", provides support for Marines, and provides community awareness programs for troop support.

Uniforms of the Marine Corps

There are "field", "dress" and "service" uniforms. Each has its own occasion and guidelines for wear (see link above for official regulations). The service uniforms include Alphas, Bravos and Charlie's. The dress blues uniforms include Alphas, Bravos, Charlie's and Deltas.

There are three field uniforms including Combat Utility, Flight Suit and Mountain Warfare. The most common is the Combat Utility, also known as MCCUU (Marine Corps Combat Utility Uniform) but it most commonly referred to as the "Utilities" or "Cammies". They are available for different uses in Forest Green and Desert Sand. The new "cammies" have a digital camouflage pattern suitable for "every clime and place".

The following is an overview of the service and dress uniform and what each includes:

Service Alphas

Dark Green Jacket

Dark Green Slacks

Long Sleeve Khaki Shirt with tie

Garrison Cover (dark green triangular cover) or Barracks Cover w/ dark green cover (round cover with black bill)

Ribbons & Shooting Badges

Service Bravos

Long Sleeve Khaki Shirt with tie

Dark Green Slacks

Garrison Cover or Barracks Cover w/ dark green cover

Ribbons

Service Charlies

Short Sleeve Khaki Shirt

White T-shirt

Dark Green Slacks

Garrison Cover or Barracks Cover w/ dark green cover

Ribbons

Dress Blue Alphas

Blues Blouse

White T-Shirt

Blue Slacks

Barracks Cover with white cover

Gloves

Medals & Ribbons

Dress Blue Bravos

Blues Blouse

White T-Shirt

Blue Slacks

Barracks Cover with white cover

Gloves

Ribbons & Shooting Badges

Dress Blue Charlies

Long Sleeve Khaki Shirt with tie

Blue Slacks

Barracks Cover with white cover

Ribbons & Shooting Badges

Dress Blue Deltas

Short Sleeve Khaki Shirt

White T-shirt

Blue Slacks

Barracks Cover with white cover

Ribbons & Shooting Badges

Marine Uniforms Versus Army and Other Branches of the Service

Marines are often confused with soldiers, who are in the United States Army. Some differences in appearance are:

Marines do not wear berets.

Marines wear boots only with the utility uniform, not other uniforms.

Marines do not salute unless they are wearing a hat (known as a "cover").

Marines do not wear covers indoors, unless they are "under arms", i.e. carrying a weapon or wearing a duty belt.

The Marine service uniform, roughly equivalent to business attire, has a khaki shirt. The equivalent Army uniform has a light-green shirt. Enlisted Marines wear their rank insignia on the sleeve of the service shirt, officers on the collar.

Army soldiers wear their rank insignia on epaulets over the shoulder.

The Marine class "A" service coat is olive green (as opposed to forest green for the Army) and has a waist-belt. The Marine service uniform is worn with either a barracks cover, which has a bill and a round top, or a garrison cover, which comes to a peak.

Marines are less generous with awards and unit identification. For example, with the exception of breast insignia denoting a few specialized qualifications such as airborne (parachute), pilot or scuba qualification, or red patches sewn on the trouser legs and covers of some logistics Marines, Marines do not normally wear any insignia or device on their utility uniforms denoting their unit, MOS (military occupational specialty), or training.

Utility uniform

Differences in the utility uniform include:

The hat (cover) of the utility uniform is constructed differently. Marine hats have eight sides and corners (hence the name "eight-point cover").

Marines wear green-colored "skivvie" undershirts with their utility uniform, even in the desert. Soldiers wear brown undershirts. (Note, as of 2004, the Marine Corps has announced the intention to switch to brown undershirts when desert camouflage is worn.)

Marines "blouse" their boots. That is, they roll the cuffs of their trousers back inside and tighten them over the boots with a cord. Soldiers either blouse their boots or tuck their trousers directly into their boots.

Marines do not wear any rank insignia or other device on the utility cover. The front of the cover has instead the Marine Corps Eagle, Globe and Anchor emblem.

On their utility uniforms, Marine officers typically wear their rank insignia on both collars, while Army officers typically wear insignia on one collar and an insignia identifying their specific "combat arm" (i.e. infantry, artillery, armor) on the other. In a garrison environment, Marine officer's insignia is usually shiny metal, and is affixed in a manner similar to a pin, while Army officers usually wear a subdued stiched on insignia. Marines used to wear black combat boots with the utility uniform, as do the Army and Air Force. But in 2002, light-brown combat boots were introduced along with a new type of camouflage, the "MARPAT" uniform. Effective 1 October 2004, black combat boots were declared obsolete and no longer authorized for general wear by Marines. Exception is made for black safety boots worn for certain tasks, such as parachuting.

Marine Corps Uniforms

Marines are not known just for their battlefield prowess, but for their unparalleled standards of professionalism and uncompromising personal conduct and appearance. It is a Marine's duty and personal obligation to maintain a professional and neat appearance. Furthermore, wearing the uniform should be a matter of personal pride to all Marines. Marines have various uniform combinations which are worn for various occasions. We've included a chart below for your reference. Note: "A" is also known as Alphas, "B" as Bravos, "C" as Charlies, and "D" as Deltas.

Uniform	Description	Occasions for Wear

Evening Dress ("A"/"B")	Dark blue w/black or dark blue trousers/skirt, enlisted wear sky blue trousers	Year-round for white tie/black tie social functions
Blue Dress "A"/"B"	Blue coat w/sky blue trousers/slacks, and dark blue skirt w/ medals ("A") or ribbons ("B")	Parades, ceremonies, formal/semi-formal social functions (winter season only unless uniformity is required)
Blue-White	Blue coat and white trousers/skirt/slacks	Parades, ceremonies,

Dress "A"/"B"	w/medals ("A") or ribbons ("B")	formal or semi-formal social functions (summer season only)
Blue Dress "C"	Khaki long-sleeve shirt and tie/black necktab w/trousers/skirt/slacks, blue sweater optional	Parades, ceremonies and uniform of the day (blue sweater worn as uniform of the day only)
Blue Dress "D"	Khaki short-sleeve shirt w/blue trousers/skirt/slacks	Parades, ceremonies

		and uniform of the day
Service "A"	Green coat and trousers/skirt/slacks w/ribbons (badges optional)	Parades, ceremonies, social events and uniform of the day
Service "B"	Khaki long-sleeve shirt w/green trousers/skirt/slacks (badges optional) Green sweater optional	Parades, ceremonies, uniform of the day (green sweater worn as uniform of the day only)
Service "C"	Khaki short-sleeve shirt w/green	Parades, ceremonies,

	trousers/skirt/slacks (badges optional) Green sweater optional	uniform of the day (green sweater worn as uniform of the day only)
Combat Utility Uniform	MARPAT desert and woodland coat and trousers (sweater or sweatshirt optional)	Working/field uniform only (woodland during winter/desert during summer season)

Physical Training Uniform	Olive green undershirt, shorts, sweatpants/shirt with a black Marine Corps emblem on the upper left trouser leg and over the left breast of the sweatshirt.	Physical training (PT) and field day

Ranks in the Marine Corps

This list is in ascending order. It includes pay grades and abbreviations in the style used by the Marine Corps.

Enlisted:

E-1, Private, Pvt

E-2, Private First Class, PFC

E-3, Lance Corporal, LCpl

Noncommissioned Officers, or NCOs:

E-4, Corporal, Cpl

E-5, Sergeant, Sgt

Staff Noncommissioned Officers, or SNCOs:

E-6, Staff Sergeant, SSgt

E-7, Gunnery Sergeant, GySgt

E-8

Master Sergeant, MSgt

First Sergeant, 1Sgt

E-9

Master Gunnery Sergeant, MGySgt

Sergeant Major, SgtMaj

Sergeant Major of the Marine Corps

NOTE 1: The E-8 and E-9 levels each have two ranks per pay grade, each with different responsibilities. Gunnery Sergeants indicate on their annual evaluations, called "fitness reports," or "fitreps" for short, their preferred promotional track: Master Sergeant or First Sergeant. The First Sergeant and Sergeant Major ranks are command-oriented, with Marines of theses ranks serving as the senior enlisted Marines in a unit, charged to assist the commanding officer in matter of discipline, administration and the morale and welfare of the unit. Master Sergeants and Master Gunnery Sergeants provide technical leadership as occupational specialists in their specific MOS. First Sergeants typically serve as the senior enlisted Marine in a company, battery or other unit at similar echelon, while Sergeants Major serve the same role in battalions, squadrons or larger units.

NOTE 2: The Sergeant Major of the Marine Corps is the senior enlisted Marine of the entire Marine Corps, personally selected by the Commandant of the Marine Corps.

Warrant Officers

W-1, Warrant Officer 1, WO1

W-2, Chief Warrant Officer 2, CWO2

W-3, Chief Warrant Officer 3, CWO3

W-4, Chief Warrant Officer 4, CWO4

W-5, Chief Warrant Officer 5, CWO5

NOTE 3: A Chief Warrant Officer, CWO2-CWO5, serving in the MOS 0306 "Infantry Weapons Officer" is designated as a special rank: "Marine Gunner". A Marine Gunner replaces the Chief Warrant Officer insignia on the right collar with a bursting bomb insignia.

Other Warrant Officers are sometimes informally also referred to as "Gunner" but this usage is not considered correct.

Commissioned officers:

Company-grade officers

O-1, Second Lieutenant, 2ndLt

O-2, First Lieutenant, 1stLt

O-3, Captain, Capt

Field-grade officers

O-4, Major, Maj

O-5, Lieutenant Colonel, LtCol

O-6, Colonel, Col

Generals

O-7, Brigadier General, BGen

O-8, Major General, MajGen

O-9, Lieutenant General, LtGen

O-10, General, Gen

NOTE 4: There has never been an O-11 "five-star" General rank thus far in the Marine Corps, though such a rank could theoretically be created at any time by an act of Congress. Currently, no officer in any branch of the U.S. military holds such a grade.

Marine Corps Structure

Marine Corps Organization

Marine Expeditionary Force (MEF): The MEF is the principal war fighting element in the active force structure of the Marine Corps and is usually commanded by a lieutenant general. The size and composition of a deployed MEF varies depending on the needs of the mission.

Marine Division: There are three Marine divisions in the active force and one in the reserve. It is the largest Marine ground combat organization of a MEF and is usually commanded by a major-general.

Marine Expeditionary Brigade (MEB): A MEB, usually led by a brigadier general, is built around a reinforced infantry regiment, an aircraft group and a Service Support Group. Capable of rapid deployment and employment via amphibious or airlift methods, it is the first echelon of a Marine Expeditionary Force.

Marine Expeditionary Unit (MEU): The smallest task force unit, the MEU has approximately 2,200 personnel and is built around a reinforced infantry battalion, a composite aircraft squadron and a support group. It is commanded by a colonel and is routinely deployed with an Amphibious Ready Group. The ground element of a MEU is a Battalion Landing Team (BLT), comprised of a reinforced infantry battalion of approximately

1,200 Marines, including three Rifle Companies. The aviation unit of a MEU is a reinforced medium helicopter squadron.

Marine Air Wing (MAW): The largest Marine aviation organization of the MEF, each MAW has a unique organizational structure and is commanded by a brigadier general.

Marine Aircraft Group (MAG): Similar to an Air Force Wing and commanded by a colonel, a MAG is the smallest aviation unit that is designed for independent operations.

The Marine Corps Birthday and Birthday Ball

The Marine Corps Birthday is one of the most celebrated traditions of the Corps. Each year on November 10th, Marines across the globe celebrate what they see as their second birthday, the day the United States Marine Corps was born. The tradition runs deep. For years Marines have been telling each other "Happy Birthday" on November 10th and attending Marine Corps Birthday balls in various cities all over the world. Each birthday, the Commandant of the Corps reads his "Birthday Message" to all Marines, and they "reflect upon the legacy of [the] Corps and upon the awesome responsibilities lying ahead." (<u>Warrior Culture of the U.S. Marines</u> by Marion F. Sturkey)

The Marine Corps Birthday is a day of pride and respect for the Corps, and it is one to be honored and celebrated.

The History

Dating back to the Phoenicians and Greeks around 500 BC, fighting men on ships have served as boarding parties and infantry while securing land bases and harbors. In 1664, the British Admiralty named its <u>soldiers of the sea</u> the "Regiment of Marines."

In the developing American colonies the new Continental Congress met at Tun Tavern in Philadelphia, Pennsylvania. On 10 November 1775 while in session in the tavern the new congress resolved:

<u>...That two Battalions of Marines be raised consisting of one Colonel, two Lieutenant</u>

<u>Colonels, two Majors & Officers as usual in other regiments; that they consist of an equal number of privates with other battalions; that particular care be taken that no person be appointed to office or enlisted into said Battalions, but such as are good seamen, or so acquainted with maritime affairs as to be able to serve to advantage by sea.</u>

These new Continental Marines set up their recruiting station in Tun Tavern. Led by their Commandant, in March 1776 they conducted their first amphibious assault against the British in the Bahamas. Continental Marines fought as naval infantry and as expeditionary forces throughout the Revolutionary War.

On 11 July 1778 the new U.S. Congress passed "An Act for Establishing and Organizing a Marine Corps":

SECTION 1: Be it enacted by the Senate of the House of Representatives of the United States of America, in Congress assembled, that in addition to the present military establishment, there shall be raised and organized a corps of marines, which shall consist of one major, four captains, sixteen first-lieutenants, twelve second-lieutenants, forty-eight sergeants, forty-eight corporals, thirty-two drums and fifes, and seven-hundred and twenty privates, including the marines who have been enlisted, or are authorized to be raised, for the naval armament, and the said corps may be formed into as many companies, or detachments, as the President of the United States shall direct, with a proper distribution of the commissioned and non-commissioned officers and musicians to each company or detachment.

This act formally established the U.S. Marine Corps. Since that time over 200 years ago, Marines have conducted over 300 assaults on foreign shores. Marines have been <u>first to fight</u> in thousands of campaigns around the world.

Marine Corps Birthday Message

In 1921, the thirteenth Commandant of the Marine Corps, MGen. John A. Lejeune, issued Marine Corps Order No. 47. This order summarized the history, mission and traditions of the Marine Corps and was to be read to all Marine commands throughout the world each year on the 10th of November. It is now referred to as the Marine Corps Birthday Message, and it is presented to Marines by the Commandant of the Marine Corps.

Marine Corps Birthday Ball

The first Marine Corps Birthday Ball took place in Philadelphia, Pennsylvania, in 1925. Like the Marine Corps itself, the Birthday Ball has evolved over the years as traditions were created, from simple origins into the polished ceremony that it is today.

Source: Warrior Culture of the U.S. Marines by Marion F. Sturkey

Women in the Marine Corps

Women Marines became a permanent part of the regular Marine Corps on 12 June 1948 when Congress passed the Women's Armed Services Integration Act (Public Law 625), but they had already proved themselves in two world wars. During World War I, Opha May Johnson was the first of 305 women to be accepted for duty in the Marine Corps Reserve on 13 August 1918. Most women filled clerical billets at Headquarters, Marine Corps to release male Marines qualified for active field service to fight in France. Other women filled jobs at recruiting stations throughout the United States. On 30 July 1919, after the war was over, orders were issued for separation of all women from the Corps.

Twenty-five years later, women were back to "free a man to fight." The Marine Corps Women's Reserve was established in February 1943. Before World War II ended, a total of 23,145 officer and enlisted women reservists served in the Corps. Unlike their predecessors, women Marines in World War II performed over 200 military assignments. In addition to clerical work, their numbers included parachute riggers, mechanics, radio operators, map makers, motor transport support, and welders. By June 1944, women reservists made up 85 percent of the enlisted personnel on duty at Headquarters, Marine Corps and almost two-thirds of the personnel manning all major posts and stations in the United States and Hawaii. Following the surrender of Japan, demobilization of the Women's Reserve proceeded rapidly, but a number of them returned to service as regulars under the 1948 Act.

In August 1950, for the first time in history, the Women Reserves were mobilized for the Korean War where the number of women Marines on active duty reached a peak strength of 2,787. Like the women of two previous wars, they stepped into stateside jobs and freed male Marines for combat duty. Women continued to serve in an expanding range of billets and by the height of the Vietnam War, there were about 2,700 women Marines on active duty serving both stateside and overseas. During this period, the Marine Corps also began opening up career-type formal training programs to women officers and advanced technical training to enlisted women. By 1975, the Corps approved the assignment of women to all occupational fields except infantry, artillery, armor and pilot/air crew. Approximately 1,000 women Marines were deployed to Southwest Asia for Operations Desert Shield and Desert Storm in 1990-1991.

Milestones for women officers include: Col Margaret A. Brewer was appointed to a general officer's billet with the rank of brigadier general becoming the first woman general officer in the history of the Corps (1978); Col Gail M. Reals became the first woman selected by a board of general officers to be advanced to brigadier general (1985); BGen Carol A. Mutter assumed command of the 3d Force Service Support Group, Okinawa, becoming the first woman to command a Fleet Marine Force unit at the flag level (1992); 2dLt Sarah Deal became the first woman Marine selected for Naval aviation training (1993); BGen Mutter became the first woman major general in the Marine Corps and the senior woman on active duty in the armed services (1994); LtGen Mutter became the first woman Marine and the second woman in the history of the armed services to wear three stars (1996); 1stLt Vernice Armour became the first female African-American combat pilot in the Marine Corps as well as any other U.S. armed service (2002).

Today, women account for 4.3 percent of all Marine officers and women make up 5.1 percent of the active duty enlisted force in the Marine Corps. These numbers continue to grow as do opportunities to serve. Ninety-three percent of all occupational fields and 62 percent of all positions are now open to women. Like their distinguished predecessors, women in the Marine Corps today continue to serve proudly and capably in whatever capacity their country and Corps requires.

Corps Respect

"Semper Fidelis" is Latin for "Always Faithful". Along with the shortened version, Semper Fi, these two phrases have been adopted as a Marine Corps slogan that is carried with all Marines for the rest of their lives. A Marine will always be a Marine; there are no ex-Marines. There are no "former Marines." Every Marine, whether serving four years or 34 years in the Corps, will remain "Always Faithful" to the Marine Corps and the core values of honor, courage and commitment.

Esprit de Corps is the attitude a recruit will learn that he or she is no longer an individual but part of a team or unit with a strong commitment to the honor of the group. A Marine does what they do for the betterment of the unit, not for themselves. Your recruit is becoming part of something bigger than him or herself and will be serving that mission above and beyond any personal agenda. Recruits become Marines who become brothers inspiring enthusiasm and devotion to the Corps.

Most of us can only stand on the sidelines and watch the transformation from recruit to Marine. Unless you have become a Marine through the grit and tough training of boot camp, you cannot possibly fully comprehend Esprit de Corps and the Core Values. However, you will come to understand that these new philosophies are not easily achieved and therefore command the greatest respect from those of us on the sidelines.

Just as your recruit son or daughter's family has grown, encompassing hundreds of new soon-to-be-Marines while in recruit training, your family is growing too. There are families across America who are standing proudly behind their recruit, watching and learning right along with them, as these young men and women succeed in their journey to become a United States Marine. Those families understand that Corps Respect can and should embrace every member of the family, not just your newly minted Marine.

The Core Values and Esprit de Corps belong to your Marine, but Corps Respect will now become part of your family values. Stand tall and take pride in knowing that your son or daughter is one of The Few, The Proud. Stand tall with your family to share in the newfound Corps Respect!

Section 3: What Your Recruit Will Go Through in Boot Camp

Recruit Training

The objective of recruit training is to produce basically trained Marines who have embraced our core values and legacy. They should be the epitome personal character, selflessness and military virtue. Every Marine should leave Parris Island with a mastery of the areas of discipline, character development, military bearing, espirit de corps, Marine Corps common combat skills and combat conditioning. Recruit training is inherently stressful for the young men and women who come to Parris Island. They will face a demanding change in lifestyle, acculturation to a military routine and a fear of the unknown. This training environment has proven to be effective for generations of

Marines. Marines who are shaped by their experiences and rigorous training are instilled with the traits to make them better citizens and prepared for the challenges of military life. Recruit training must remain demanding, formal, and challenging in order to achieve the desired end state: making a basic Marine. These basic Marines must be instilled with the discipline to obey orders, respect authority, and uphold our warrior ethos.

Yellow Footprints

The yellow footprints are one of the first things new recruits will see when they get to boot camp. The yellow footprints are just that, yellow footprints on the concrete. Several in a row that recruits are to stand on when they first get off of the bus. This act is steeped in tradition. It is an honor to be able to stand where so many before stood. The yellow footprints serve as a symbol of the 13 weeks of grueling training ahead. The footprints are something your recruit may have heard about if they have been thinking of enlisting in the Marine Corps. The first thing they will see when they arrive is a drill instructor who will board the bus and proceed to yell at recruits to get off of the bus. Your recruit will be instructed to step on the yellow footprints which form a formation that will have them and the other new recruits ready to enter the building.

Chaos will follow as several recruits, including your recruit, are scrambling to get your stuff, get off the bus and get on the yellow footprints. Your recruit will not do much of anything right, just so you know, but they must always try.

Head and eyes to the front. Stand at the position of attention. As your recruit is standing on the infamous yellow footprints, it is at this time that they will be asking themselves, "what have I gotten myself into?" This is because they are being screamed at by drill instructors who are giving them their first taste of how the next 13 weeks will be. My advice would be for your recruit to do exactly as they are told, as fast as possible. This advice should be followed throughout their training to avoid punishment and embarrassment, although nothing is really going to help them avoid either. Your recruit will be broken down and rebuilt into a Marine, if they are lucky.

Your recruit will never forget the yellow footprints, even after they graduate boot camp. It is a tradition that many Marines who have gone before them have also done. Your recruit will be able to feel the history when they step on the yellow footprints where thousands before them have stepped. Some have even fought and died for this country. All are heroes. All have stepped on the yellow footprints.

Drill Instructors

Only about 600 drill instructors shape the approximately 20,000 recruits who come to Parris Island annually into basic United States Marines. This handful of dedicated DIs are trusted with sustaining a more than 237-year legacy by transforming men and women into the next generation of Marines.

HISTORY OF THE CAMPAIGN COVER

The introduction of the pre-World War II campaign or field hat worn by drill instructors today originated during an advisory council meeting in 1956. Senior noncommissioned officers strongly recommended the adoption of better "headgear" for DI's. At that time, the khaki barracks cap had a bill, but didn't shade the eyes. The soft khaki garrison cap didn't have a bill, and the green herringbone cape worn with the field uniform was also inadequate in the summer sun. The pith helmet was a practical alternative for wear in the hot Carolina summer. It was cool and its wide brim provided good shade for the eyes and neck. It later became the hat used by marksmanship instructors at the rifle range.

Further study indicated that the field hat was the item most preferred by DIs. It shaded the neck and eyes well, but did not keep the head as cool as the pith helmet. The field hat was a bit of tradition going back to the "Old Corps" of pre-World War II days. It also was more suitable for year-round wear than the pith helmet. By early June 1956, the Depot had requisitioned 1,000 field hats for delivery on Sept. 1, 1956, but Gen. Wallace M. Greene Jr., wanted to order 700 hats immediately. On Saturday, July 21, 1956, at 7:30 a.m. all 603 drill instructors of the recruit training command obtained their new hats.

Female drill instructors authorized to wear "Smokey"
The commandant of the Marine Corps announced on Sept. 13, 1996, that all female drill instructors were authorized to wear the previously male-only "Smokey" field hat. The commandant's decision has answered the frequently asked question, "Why not?" It was first asked in 1976 when the first females graduated from Drill Instructor School and again in 1983 when female DIs began wearing their scarlet shoulder cord. During their Sept. 26, 1996, graduation ceremony, female DI School graduates were issued field hats. A cord retirement ceremony took place Oct. 2, 1996, after which female DIs ceased wearing the scarlet cord and began wearing the cover. The commandant, Gen. Charles C. Krulak, was on hand for the event.

The final scarlet shoulder cord, the previous symbol of a female DI, was placed in the Parris Island Museum.

DRILL INSTRUCTORS' CREED

"These recruits are entrusted to my care.
I will train them to the best of my ability.
I will develop them into smartly disciplined,
physically fit, basically trained Marines,
thoroughly indoctrinated in love
of Corps and country.
I will demand of them, and demonstrate by my
own example, the highest standards of personal
conduct, morality and professional skill."

Practical Application and Written Testing

Recruits spend a great deal of time in the classroom during recruit training and, during weeks 10 and 11 of boot camp, they must prove they have retained the abundance of information they were taught. Recruits must perform a Final Practical Application Test, as well as a Final Written Academic Test.

Final Practical Application Test

The final practical application test is a series of test events in which recruits are required to demonstrate their knowledge and mastery of the subject.

These areas include:

First Aid skills

Customs and Courtesies (like saluting or boarding a ship)

Marine Corps Uniform and rank identification

Weapons assembly and disassembly

Final Written Academic Test

The final written academic test is the second of two written tests recruits take during their training. Recruits must pass both the practical application test and the written test in order to progress in training and to be able to graduate. Recruits are tested across the spectrum of what they have been taught in training.

Test material includes:

Core values and ethics

First Aid

Military History

Customs and Courtesies

Marine Corps Uniforms

Leadership

Marine Corps Policy and Organization

BWT (Basic Warrior Training) subjects like land navigation and hand and arm signals

Marksmanship

MRP: Medical Rehabilitation Platoon

Medical Rehabilitation Platoon, or MRP, is the platoon that recruits are assigned to if they are injured or become ill during recruit training. Recruits may become ill or injured. Your recruit will be given the best medical care available, with doctors and teams of hospital personnel to assure your recruit is well-cared for and getting the medical attention s/he needs. There will be no expense to the recruit for medical procedures or prescriptions. S/he will continue to receive full pay for time spent in MRP.

You may get a short phone call from your recruit if s/he has been assigned to MRP. You'll certainly have additional questions at this time. Your best source for official information about a recruit in MRP, particularly if s/he has just been assigned to MRP, is your son or daughter's recruiter. In situations where your recruit's recovery time will be extended, you may be given a contact person at the Depot. You may also be given a new mailing address to send mail. For extended stays in MRP, small care packages with appropriate items are acceptable.

Some terminology that may be used in MRP follows:

PEB: Physical Evaluation Board

STC: Special Training Company

PCP: Physical Training Company

BMP: Basic Military Platoon

RSP: Recruit Separation Platoon

FSRP: Female Recruit Separation Platoon

EHP: Evaluation Holding Platoon

RTFD: Return To Full Duty

MCMAP & Pugil Sticks

MCMAP - <u>Marine Corps Martial Arts Program</u>
From its inception in 1775, the Marine Corps has distinguished itself as a Martial Culture. The legacy of our Corps is built upon the close combat of ships of sail, the storming of the bois de Belleau, and the holding of "Bloody Ridge" on Guadalcanal. Drawing upon our rich tradition of promoting values and our warrior ethos, the Marine Corps developed the Marine Corps Martial Arts Program or MCMAP. It is a martial art that was designed to be, and is the "synergy of mental, character, and physical disciplines."

MCMAP is based on five, colored-belt levels with six different degrees of Black. Each belt level is broken down into three disciplines, each of which a Marine must become proficient in before attaining the next belt level. The mental, character, and physical disciplines of the warrior are the foundation of the Martial Arts Program. The mental discipline consists of warrior studies, martial culture studies, combative behavior studies, and other professional military education. The character discipline is built around the Marine Corps' core values: Honor, Courage, and Commitment. The character discipline stresses the role of the warrior on and off the battlefield. The physical discipline consists of the techniques taught at each belt level.

Through the successful synergy of these disciplines at each belt level, a Marine will enhance their own warrior spirit. Recruits are introduced to the fundamentals of MCMAP on training day one and progress towards the final test to earn their Tan Belt. The Tan Belt syllabus teaches recruits basic MCMAP techniques, is an introduction to the martial culture, and form the basis for all further MCMAP instruction.

Pugil Sticks

A pugil stick is a heavily padded training weapon used by military personnel for bayonet training since the 1930s or 1940s. Similar to a quarterstaff, the pugil stick may be marked at one end to indicate which portion represents the bayonet proper and which the butt of the rifle.

Pugil bouts are usually conducted with hard contact while wearing protective gear such as football helmets, flak jackets, groin protectors, and gloves. Many recruits have never experienced the realities of inter-personal violence found in close combat, and pugil sticks provide effective, but safe, "full contact" combative training at the entry level. It is also an effective tool for enhancing the endurance and improvisation that are building blocks to developing the physical skills and mental toughness vital to success on the battlefield.

Marine Week
Training days 66-69 make up Marine Week; this is the last and final week of Recruit Training. Marine Week is a period of time where the new Marines learn to operate in a

more decentralized environment. After eleven weeks of being told what to do almost every waking moment, this is a chance for them to show their drill instructors what they have learned about small unit leadership, ethics, and core values. They are not recruits any more, they are allowed to wear a watch, to move about the Depot as small units, and are now addressed by their rank and last name, or simply as "Marine." Drill instructors make a transition as well, serving more as mentors, and the new Marines call them by their rank and last name. There is also an important moment when Marines, past and present, come visit and "Share the Legacy," passing along their experiences, and telling the new Marines how the Corps' core values have shaped their lives.

Initial Drill Evaluation

The Initial Drill Evaluation tests each platoon's ability to listen to the orders of its Drill Instructor at this point in training, and is a demonstration of the unit's degree of discipline and esprit de corps. Drill is used as one of the first methods of transforming these recruits from civilians into Marines, and plays a large part on their development of teamwork and unit cohesion. The object of close order drill is to teach Marines, through exercise, to obey orders immediately and in the correct manner. Close order drill is one foundation of discipline and esprit de corps. Additionally, it has long been, and remains, one of the finest methods for developing confidence and troop-leadership abilities in lower-ranking Marines.

Classroom Training

New recruits have much to learn and, therefore, spend a great deal of time in the classroom during recruit training. Recruits in Marine Corps boot camp take classes covering subjects such as Customs and Courtesies, First Aid, Marine Corps History, USMC Mission and Organization, Terrorism Awareness, USMC Leadership, Official Policies and Organizational Values, and Operational Risk Management. For more information on some of these categories, see the sections below.

Customs and Courtesies – New recruits are introduced to the customs and courtesies of the Marine Corps. They learn things that no Marine forgets. That the official motto of the Marine Corps, "Semper Fidelis," is Latin for "Always

Faithful," and that it is sometimes abbreviated, "Semper Fi." They learn to describe and state the significance of the Marine Corps emblem. They learn all three verses of the Marines Hymn. They also learn the background of the terms: Leatherneck, Devil Dog, and First to Fight.

First Aid – First Aid refers to the medical measures a Marine can carry out for him/herself or for his or her fellow Marines before emergency treatment can be provided by a corpsman or a doctor. Corpsmen and doctors can't be every place at once, and there may be a time when a Marine will have to depend upon his or her own knowledge to save his or her own life or that of a fellow Marine. Recruits learn and are tested on basic first aid tactics such as

CPR, basic lifesaving steps, how to transport a casualty, how to stop bleeding, and how to identify poisonous animals and insects.

Marine Corps History – The basis for being a Marine and contributing to its rich tradition is understanding how the Marine Corps came to be, what it has done, and why our history is so important to us. Recruits learn that since 1775, the United States Marine Corps has served honorably and proudly whenever and wherever our Nation has asked it to, and today's Marine Corps stands ready to continue in the proud tradition of those who so valiantly fought and died at Belleau Wood, Iwo Jima, the Chosin Reservoir, and Khe Sanh, among others. They learn that Marine history is replete with accounts of Marines who have shown exceptional bravery and made extraordinary sacrifices, and that, almost without exception, those accounts of heroism and service can be described by the words "Honor, Courage, and Commitment," -- the Marine Corps' core values. Those three words succinctly describe the reason Marines have always been looked upon as a fighting force without equal, capable of exceptional accomplishment in the face of insurmountable odds.

Terrorism Awareness – During this class, instructors discuss the definition of terrorism, terrorism operations, and self-protection from terrorist attacks.

USMC Leadership – Every Marine is, or will be, a leader at some point in his or her career, and leadership development begins early in the recruit process. Recruits will learn and practice the eleven Leadership Principles, such as "Know Yourself and Seek Self-Improvement," "Know Your Marines and Look Out For Their Welfare," and, "Set the Example." They will also learn and practice the fourteen Marine Corps Leadership Traits: Dependability, Bearing, Courage, Decisiveness, Endurance, Enthusiasm, Initiative, Integrity, Judgment, Justice, Knowledge, Tact, Unselfishness, and Loyalty.

Haircuts & Hygiene

It is not uncommon to hear a statement like, "Marines sure do look sharp in uniform!" As a matter of fact, some Marines claim part of their motivation to join the Marine Corps was found in the desire to attain the honor of wearing the esteemed uniform. Why do Marines look so sharp in uniform? The answer lies in their incredible attention to detail and strict uniform regulations which include specifications regarding haircuts and hygiene.

Recruits learn the importance of these regulations early on in boot camp as one of their first stops on the depot is the barber shop. Throughout the course of recruit training recruits continue to learn about their newfound uniform regulations and the standards they will be held to as a Marine. Marine Corps grooming standards specify, in thorough detail, regulations regarding haircuts, hair styles, hair colors, facial hair, jewelry, eyeglasses, dental ornamentation, cosmetics, fingernails and more. Additional uniform regulations include orders against doing any of the following while walking in uniform: chewing gum, using a cell phone, or placing hands in pockets.

Every Marine is a Rifleman

"Every Marine a rifleman," no matter what their Military Occupational Specialty has been one of the hallmarks of the Marine Corps throughout our history. From the Marine marksmen shooting from the high rigging on ships during the sea battles of the American Revolution, to the battle of Belleau Wood, France in June of 1918 during World War I where Marines hit German targets from more than 500 yards away, to Gunnery Sergeant Carlos Hathcock, a Marine sniper in Vietnam with a service record of 93 confirmed kills, we have set ourselves apart by our shooting prowess.

To develop those skills recruits will spend two weeks learning how to shoot the Marine Corps way. The first week is called Grass Week where recruits learn the fundamentals and positions they will use. The second week is Firing Week where recruits will practice, and then qualify on the Table 1 course of fire, or the Known Distance (KD) course with the M16A2 service rifle.

Recruits fire the same M16A2 service rifle that they were issued at the beginning of training and have been carrying every day for the last five weeks. The M16A2 is a 5.56 mm, Lightweight, Magazine fed, Gas operated, Air cooled, Shoulder fired weapon. Recruits learn to remember these characteristics of the by the acronym LM-GAS. The M16A2 is constructed of steel, aluminum and composite plastics.

Four Rifle Range Safety Rules

The Rifle Range

This is My Rifle. There Are Many like it but This One is Mine

First and foremost, a Marine is a rifleman. Unlike other branches of the military, every Marine is trained and qualified as a rifleman first. Although a Marine may have one of many jobs in the Marine Corps, every Marine knows how to fire his or her rifle. In Marine Corps boot camp, your recruit will be taught basic rifle marksmanship. If your recruit has never shot a weapon before, the Marine Corps will to teach them how. It is almost better if your recruit has no experience because the Marine Corps will teach them the way they want them to shoot without any prior knowledge getting in the way.

Recruits will march from the barracks they have called home for several weeks to the rifle range barracks where they will stay for two weeks. During that time, all recruits will learn how to not only fire their rifle but how to qualify during live fire exercises. Recruits will learn how to fire their weapons from sitting, standing and prone positions. Classes will be given by PMI's, or Primary Marksmanship Instructors on how to use the weapon's sites to correctly fire the rifle. Recruits will be given range safety classes and will learn the rules of how to conduct themselves while on the range. This is no laughing matter. Your recruit must listen and follow directions. On the final days of rifle range training, your recruit will try to qualify with a passing score. There are three badges that the Marine Corps offers based on the recruit's performance. Qualification requirements are as follows:

220-250 Expert

210-219 Sharpshooter

190-209 Marksman

If recruits fail to qualify, they will be given an additional opportunity the following week during team week to qualify. Instead of joining their platoon on team week, they will be at the range trying to qualify.

Recruits must qualify from different firing position and from different firing distances of 200, 300, and 500 yard lines. In addition to knowing how to fire their rifle, your recruit must know how to clean it. Plenty of time will be given to recruits to clean their rifle. Any lull in training will be filled with cleaning their rifle. For those who enjoy shooting weapons, this will be a positive experience. For those who are apprehensive and have never fired a weapon, it is important to remember to listen carefully and asked questions when allowed to do so. Your recruit will have coaches there that will help them, so that they do not get flustered.

Grass Week & Shooting Positions

Recruits are introduced to the four shooting positions during Grass Week, training days 30-34. A Combat Marksmanship Instructor, or CMI, teaches recruits the fundamentals of weapons safety and marksmanship with their M-16A2 service rifle. During this week, recruits become familiar with the following shooting positions:

Sitting

Prone

Kneeling

Standing

Recruits learn how to fire, how to adjust their sights and how to take into account the effects of wind and weather. They spend hours in the four positions, preparing their bodies to remain steady while they shoot.

Recruits will also "zero" their service rifle and fire a grouping exercise to verify how their individual rifle shoots. The results will tell the recruit the initial sight settings. By the time a recruit fires that first actual shot during Firing Week, he or she will have dry-fired his or her rifle from each of the four positions thousands of times.

Firing Week & Qualification Day (Qual Day)

Qualification Day (Qual Day) is the last day of Firing Week during recruit training. During Firing Week, the second week of marksmanship training, recruits begin before sunrise, preparing their rifles and themselves to shoot the known-distance course of fire. Recruits prepare for rifle qualification day by firing rounds of both slow fire (one shot at a time) and rapid fire (10 shots in a row). Recruits fire from four shooting positions at ranges of 200, 300, and 500 yards. As recruits practice shooting, they are assisted and evaluated by their Combat Marksmanship Instructor, their Coach, and their drill instructors. All are working to assist the recruit to ensure that the fundamentals have been learned, and that each recruit shoots the best that he or she can. On Qual Day all recruits are trying to shoot their best and are striving for the coveted "Crossed Rifles" of the Rifle Expert badge. Recruits can also earn the Rifle Sharpshooter and Rifle Marksman badges.

Confidence and "O" Courses

The **"O"Course**, or obstacle course, is a corner stone of the Combat Conditioning program. All recruits run the obstacle course several times during recruit training. The course challenges the recruit's upper body strength as well as their technique on the course. The obstacle course proves that brute strength alone is not enough to quickly negotiate the course. Those recruits that work on technique find the course easier to run. The **Confidence Course**, as its name implies, is designed to build the self-confidence of the recruit. The recruit develops physically and mentally by overcoming obstacles that require strength, balance, and determination. The Confidence Course consists of eleven obstacles, designed so that each obstacle is more physically challenging then the last. The Confidence Course is a great morale builder, as most of the recruits find out that after a little practice, they can negotiate the obstacles with ease. Recruits receive additional instruction on the values of the Corps which are further elaborated and detailed.

Discipline

Bearing

Loyalty

Flexibility

Esprit de Corps

Teamwork

Commitment

Dependability

Self Confidence

Self-Improvement

Aggressiveness

Pride

Health and Wellness During Boot Camp

From Health and Wealth to Religious Ministries

Recruits in Marine Corps boot camp receive the best training possible and are very well cared for throughout the course of their thirteen weeks on the Recruit Depot.

From injury prevention and dental treatment to recruit pay and the Thrift Savings Plan, every base is covered, including Religious Ministries.

Injury Prevention

The Marine Corps' Sports Medicine Injury Prevention program is in place during recruit training to ensure this rigorous training is completed with as few musculoskeletal injuries as possible.

Specialist in the fields of physical conditioning and injury prevention are part of the recruit training staff. These experts coupled with the Navy's Medical Personnel on Parris Island, provide a force so that the physical training can remain demanding with minimal injury risk.

Note: Recruits also receive a dental exam and, when needed, some dental treatment during recruit training.

Thrift Savings Plan

Recruits receive a class on the Thrift Savings Plan, or TSP. The TSP is a Federal Government-sponsored retirement savings and investment plan that the U.S. Congress established in the Federal Employees' Retirement System Act of 1986. The purpose of the TSP is to provide retirement income. TSP is a defined contribution plan, and the amount of retirement income that you receive from your TSP account will depend on how much you have contributed to your account during your working years and the earnings on those contributions. The TSP offers the same type of savings and tax benefits that many private corporations offer their employees under so - called "401(k)" plans.

Religious Ministries

An Integral part of making, and being a Marine, is individual spiritual readiness. Recruits are provided the opportunity, if they desire, to worship within their individual faith or beliefs. They also learn about religious tolerance, ethical awareness, and how spiritual readiness is a part of their personal understanding and ownership of core Values. The functions of the Recruit Training Ministry are:

Conducting worship services.

Pastoral Counseling.

Stress Management Counseling.

Assisting in the teaching of core values classes.

Delivering messages from the Red Cross.

Combat Water Survival

By definition, the Marine Corps is an amphibious assault force. Therefore all Marine recruits are required to know how to survive in the water. Recruits face many challenges during their 13 weeks on the recruit depot, but swim week is especially challenging for recruits who don't know how to swim. Training in combat water survival develops a recruit's confidence in the water. Recruits receive basic water survival training at the indoor pool, which is safely conducted by specially-trained instructors.

A new qualification system for combat water survival was implemented on November 10, 2010, that coincides with new combat and battlefield needs. The new system will train recruits to be able to survive in the water while wearing all of their combat gear (including a rifle, helmet, flak jacket and pack), whereas the old system only required recruits to train in their camouflage utility uniform. Instead of the previous six qualification levels, there are now three: basic, intermediate and advanced. All recruits must now be qualified at the basic level, which teaches full combat gear shedding, instead of achieving Combat Water Survival-4 (CWS-4), which was the minimum requirement of the old water survival program. However, recruits may choose to progress beyond the basic level.

Combat Conditioning

The Combat Conditioning program for recruits at the Marine Corps Recruit Depots serves as an introduction to strenuous activity for many recruits. Recruits will conduct Combat Conditioning exercises almost every other day during recruit training. The program has, as its goals, not only success as measured by the Marine Corps Physical Fitness Test, or PFT, but also those physical skills necessary to excel in a modern military environment and in combat. The focus is on functional exercises, and uses a progressive method to build a strong foundation in general fitness. The program increases core strength and upper body development through power movements and events like the obstacle and confidence course, MCMAP (Marine Corps Martial Arts Program), and 3, 5, 6, 7.5 mile conditioning hikes with individual load bearing equipment. Conditioning hikes increase the recruit's stamina and confidence.

The Crucible

The Crucible is the final test before a recruit is awarded the Eagle, Globe and Anchor and for the first time called a Marine. The Crucible is meant to test the mental and physical strength and endurance of each recruit. It is tested by a series of games and challenges in which recruits must work together. This is enhanced by sleep deprivation and limited food. Each recruit is given four MREs which must be self-rationed. There are recruits who eat their rations early and suffer hunger later on. Don't be one of them. The Crucible begins by marching out to the area. This is a long march in itself. The march home is going to be about 10 miles and it is done in formation carrying your ruck sack and rifle. Blisters and sore feet are common so it is imperative to take care of your feet while in boot camp. That means changing your socks when you are told to do so and using moleskin to cover any blisters. Recruits will get maybe a total of 8 hours sleep over the three days of the Crucible. They will camp out with a makeshift tent and a thin piece of plastic foam mat which is rolled up and also carried on their backs. Remember, this is three days without a shower. It's going to be all kinds of smelly. Recruits will also still be required to perform fire watch duties in rotation.

The Crucible is the final test of each recruit. It is designed to reveal leaders and test each recruit's stamina and endurance. The object is to work together. Recruits will either succeed or fail but they will do it together. In fact, all of the challenges will require teamwork to successfully solve the challenges.

Section 4: Graduation

Preparing for Graduation
Shopping and Restaurants

On family day and graduation day, you may shop or dine at certain establishments on the Depots without a military ID.

What to Wear to Graduation

Dress comfortably and wear very comfortable walking shoes. Have a sweater or jacket for colder seasons. Many families wear graduation T-shirts on family day with their recruits battalion and color on it. Many prefer to dress less casually on graduation day, but that does not mean formal attire. Business casual is perfectly acceptable. Remember, you'll be sitting on the viewing stands, which are bleachers. You'll have to "climb" the bleachers, so mothers may prefer not to wear skirts, dresses or high-heeled shoes. You'll have to walk quite a bit. Dress neatly and comfortably.

What to Bring With You

Bring sunscreen and use it. The viewing stands have no protection from the sun, and, even on a cloudy day, you can get sunburned. Bring a stroller for younger children.

Bring a photo ID for every family member except young children. If you will be driving onto the Depot, you must have proof of vehicle registration and insurance.

Taking Photos/Videos

You may take photos and videos of The Depot, the moto run, family day, the museum, the buildings, and graduation. There are areas of the Depot that are restricted access. You cannot take photos or videos in those areas nor can those areas be accessed on family day and graduation day.

Group Visits

Groups visiting Parris Island who wish an organized, escorted tour must submit a request at least 40 days prior to arriving. Group tours will be granted on a case-by-case basis and is contingent on factors such as manpower and time, as well as government regulations. Visits are typically limited to Mondays through Fridays. Eligible groups include JROTC, ROTC, reunion groups, community organizations, veterans' organizations, active duty military groups/units, etc.

Miscellaneous Information Regarding Group Tours

Transportation

Transportation to, from and around Parris Island must be provided by the group. Military vehicles will not be authorized. All vehicle operators must be licensed and possess registration and proof on insurance for their vehicles.

Lodging

Lodging for most groups is not available on Parris Island. The use of military barracks or other military buildings for overnight lodging is only available to ROTC, JROTC and Young Marines groups and is granted on a space-available basis.

Meals

Groups may request to eat at most base dining facilities, including a mess hall. Options and costs will be coordinated by the group and Parris Island after the request form is submitted.

For all ROTC/JROTC groups, mess hall meals and Meals, Ready-to-Eat are provided to students at no cost. Chaperones/instructors/staff will pay the full government meal rate (Breakfast $2.50; Lunch $4.60; Dinner $4.60).

For all Young Marines groups, mess hall meals and Meals, Ready-to-Eat are provided to children at the reduced government meal rate (Breakfast $2.10; Lunch $3.95; Dinner $3.95).

Chaperones/instructors/staff will pay the full government meal rate (Breakfast $2.50; Lunch $4.60; Dinner $4.60).

For more information, contact the Parris Island visits section at 843-228-3349.

Lodging

On Base Facilities:

Lodging on base is available to the families at a very reasonable rate; however, there are a very limited number of rooms available. Please call in advance to the numbers listed below to reserve your room.

Osprey Inn (On Base)

Marine Corps Recruit Depot, Parris Island

843-228-2744 (Reservations) | 843-228-3962 (Front Desk)

If there is no available lodging, try the DeTreville House (below).

DeTreville House

Marine Corps Air Station, Beaufort

843-522-1663

Note: The Deville House is not on Parris Island. It is approximately 10 miles away.

F.A.Q.s

Q: Where can I find a listing of hotels and motels?

A: The Beaufort Regional Chamber of Commerce provides an extensive list of local and national chain accommodations. They can be reached at 800-638-3525.

Q: Can I stay on the base?

A: Yes. Osprey Inn is located on Parris Island. The Osprey Inn provides temporary housing primarily for military personnel on temporary additional duty. Nonmilitary personnel visiting recruits may stay as guests at the Osprey Inn on space-available basis. Reservations can be made 15 days prior to the graduation date starting at 8 a.m. For reservations, please call 843-228-2744 or 843-228-3962.

Q: Are there other military bases in the area in which I can stay?

A: Yes, The DeTreville House is a temporary lodging facility on Marine Corps Air Station Beaufort, located approximately 15 minutes from Parris Island. All rooms are equipped with private bath, A/C unit, TV/VCR/HBO, microwave, refrigerator, coffeepot, iron and ironing board, alarm clock, hair dryer, data ports, smoke detector, wireless internet service and full housekeeping service. Rollaway beds available at front desk for $5 per night and cribs at no charge. Handicap accessible rooms are available. Nonmilitary personnel visiting recruits may stay as guests on space-available basis. For reservations, please call 843-522-1663.

Professional Photos and Videos Taken of Recruits During Boot Camp

During boot camp, recruits will have their photos taken with their platoon as well as individually in the "dress blues" uniform. A video of graduation will also be produced, and that video will include footage from each battalion. Both Parris Island and San Diego offer these services. Your recruit will be given an opportunity to purchase the photos as well as the video. They will also be given the opportunity to order a yearbook, and at Parris Island, that will be the only time the yearbooks are available for order. Individual photos will be given to the recruit prior to Family day, but will not be mailed home. Recruits who miss photo day for any reason or recruits who must have retakes will have those photos mailed to them. When a recruit has his/her photo taken and then has to change companies because he/she was set back in the graduation cycle, the photos are sent to his/her new platoon.

Parris Island Photos

Parris Island recruits should order the individual photos and yearbooks during boot camp. The individual photos can be ordered later by calling the Recruit Photo office at (843) 228-1555 – they should be available for a period of four years.

Parris Island Yearbooks

Only recruits can order yearbooks. Family members cannot call and order one even if their recruit is in boot camp. Recruits will be able to order a yearbook on TD (training day) 26. That is the one and only time that they will be able to order a yearbook. No orders will be taken after that date. If you would like to have a yearbook please send your recruit a reminder in a letter (prior to TD 26) to order one.

Parris Island Graduation and Marine Corps Videos

The Parris Island graduation video, "Making Marines: the Change is Forever", can be ordered by the recruit during training and will also be available on Family Day and Graduation day at the Douglas Visitor's Center. The producers of this film, "Good-To-Go Video", have archived copies of Parris Island Graduation VHS tapes dating back to November 1999. Parris Island Marines that graduated on or after May 23, 2003 can purchase DVD copies of their graduation.

Good-To-Go Video

P.O. Box 996

Beaufort, SC 29901

800-889-6734

"Good-To-Go Video" is proud to bring to you high quality, entertaining video products that focus exclusively on the United States Marine Corps. Powerful, fast-paced, and fully charged with a ferocious patriotic spirit, our videos will show you what it takes to become a Marine, then what it's like to BE a Marine. We'll also provide some insight as to why all Marines are

<u>so fiercely proud of their history and traditions and why they possess such a unique love of Country and Corps.</u>

San Diego Photos

Recruits, when ordering the individual "dress blues" photo, may also order a yearbook/graduation book as well as a slideshow DVD. This DVD is different than the graduation video. It is a slideshow of candid still shots taken of the recruits throughout all phases of training. These should be ordered by the recruit during training, but you may order copies of them afterward through the Marine Corps Community Service website or by calling the yearbook office at (619) 296-3840. The yearbook office keeps records for two years. For books older than 4 years, you can contact the MCRD Historical Society (619) 524-4426.

San Diego Graduation Videos

In San Diego, the producers of the video also put the platoon footage online for the parents, family and friends back home to review. Generally, this video is filmed on the Friday two weeks prior to graduation, but there is no set timetable for when the footage is taken or available. There are also times when some platoons are not filmed due to scheduling conflicts. The video shows a close-up of each recruit as they stand on a platform. At this time, there is no similar service for photos or videos to be previewed prior to graduation for recruits at Parris Island.

Link to MCRD San Diego Recruit Platoon Videos:

www.DevilDogs.info

1st Battalion

Alpha Company

Bravo Company

Charlie Company

Delta Company

2nd Battalion

Echo Company

Fox Company

Golf Company

Hotel Company

3rd Battalion

India Company

Kilo Company

Lima Company

Mike Company

The San Diego graduation video, <u>Pass in Review</u> is produced by David James Productions. The video includes the Eagle, Globe and Anchor ceremony, the Moto Run, Liberty formation on Family Day and the Graduation ceremony. Also included are the platoon videos which they so generously provide for parents to view during boot camp.

David James Productions

P.O. Box 84166

San Diego, CA 92138

(619) 725-6296

If ordered during boot camp, the <u>Pass In Review</u> video usually arrives within 2 weeks of graduation. Yearbooks and/or the slideshow DVD can take up to 4 months to be delivered.

Parris Island Family Orientation

Family and friends of Marine Corps Recruits are strongly encouraged to attend the graduation ceremonies for the announcement that your Recruit has earned the respected title of United States Marine. Graduation is three-part: Wednesday is Family Orientation Day, Thursday is Family Day and Graduation is Friday. The Marine Corps has activities planned for all three days. Plan to arrive in Parris Island by Tuesday evening before Family Orientation Day. You and your new Marine can depart immediately after the graduation ceremony on Friday. The nearest major airports to Parris Island are the Savannah/Hilton Head

International Airport (SAV) and the Hilton Head Airport (HHH). The next closest airport is the Charleston International Airport (CHS). Transportation to and from these airports is not provided, however both airports have rental car agencies.

There is no limit to the number of guests the new Marines may have on the Depot for the Family Days or Graduation. Dress is casual but remember you will be walking around with your soon-to-be Marine and attending sessions and meet and greets on Wednesday and Thursday, so dress accordingly. Bare midriffs would be inappropriate. Very comfortable walking shoes for all family members are a requirement on both days. Wheelchairs are available free of charge at the Douglas Visitor's Center.

You'll want to arrive early each day at the Depot to avoid long lines at the gate. For activities to do on the Depot, see dining, shopping and entertainment at the bottom of this page for restaurants, shops and hours of operation.

Important Note: Due to some holidays, including, but not limited to, Easter, Thanksgiving, and Christmas, a handful of graduating classes will graduate on a Wednesday with Family Day on Tuesday and Family Orientation Day on Monday. The same schedule will apply; substitute Monday, Tuesday and Wednesday (graduation day) for Wednesday, Thursday and Friday in the schedule below.

Changes in the levels of security alerts could alter scheduled events. Maps of the Depot, parking passes and the schedule of events can be obtained at the Douglas Visitor's Center.

Family Orientation Day

9:00 am-4:00 pm - Family Check-in at the Douglas Visitors' Center; Java Café open 9:00 am - 12:00 pm

10:00 am-12:30 pm - Marine Corps 101, including a "Behind the Scenes" tour, at Douglas Visitors' Center

Lunch - Traditions (Officer/SNCO Club), Food Court, Subway, Golf Course

2:30 pm-4:30 pm - Family Orientation Brief at the Lyceum

4:00 pm - Meet & Greet at Traditions (Officer/SNCO Club)

5:00 pm-8:00 pm - Steak Night at Traditions (Officer/SNCO Club). Reservations required.

Family Day

Please register before 9:50 a.m. at the Douglas Visitor Center.

6:30 a.m. - Java Café open in Visitor Center

7:00 a.m. - Motivational Run

9:30 a.m. - Battalion Commander's Brief describing Recruit Training in the All-Weather Training Facility

9:50 a.m. - Liberty Ceremony (on base liberty commences upon conclusion of the ceremony)

10:00 a.m.-3:00 p.m. - Barracks Open House

10:00 a.m.-3:00 p.m. - Observation of events at Leatherneck Square

3:00 p.m. - Liberty Ends

Graduation Day

The Morning Colors Ceremony (flag raising) with musical accompaniment by the Parris

Island Marine Band is held Friday at 7:45 a.m. in front of Barrow Hall.

Graduation is held Friday mornings at 9:00 a.m. on the Depot's Peatross Parade Deck and lasts about an hour. In the event of inclement weather, graduation ceremonies will be held in two or three indoor locations, which will be announced on the morning of graduation at the Douglas Visitor's Center.

Dining Services on the Depot

Food Court

Primo's Express

Habanero

Java Café - Inside the MCX

Parris Island Food Court is open Monday-Saturday 6:00 a.m. – 8:00 p.m. & Sunday 7:00 a.m. – 8:00 p.m. Serving Mexican food, pizza, and delicious hot and cold sandwiches - eat in or take-out available.

Restaurants

Subway (open 10:00 a.m. to 10:00 p.m.)

Sand Trap Grill & Café (open 7:00 a.m. to 6:00 p.m.)

Four Winds Restaurant / Bar

Family Day Lunch Buffet – all you can eat southern fried chicken, spaghetti, salad bar, cake and beverage. Adults $10, Children $5, Under 5 Free! Graduating Marines eat free! 10:30 a.m. to 3:00 p.m.

Brig & Brew (Thursday, 10:00 a.m. to 10:00 p.m.)

Shopping Services on the Depot

Marine Corps Exchange open Monday-Saturday 6:00 a.m. to 10:00 p.m. and Sunday 7:00 a.m. to 10:00 p.m.

7 Day Store (gas & convenience store) open Monday-Saturday 6:00 a.m. to 10:00 p.m. and Sunday 7:00 a.m. to 10:00 p.m.

4th Battalion Weapons & Exchange open Monday-Friday 8:00 a.m. to 5:30 p.m.

Museum Gift Shop open daily 10:00 a.m. to 4:30 p.m.

GNC open Monday-Saturday 9:00 a.m. to 7:00 p.m. and Sunday 10:00 a.m. to 6:00 p.m.

Recreation on the Depot

Movie Theatre

Bowling

Legends Golf Course

San Diego Family Day and Graduation

Family and friends are strongly encouraged to attend the graduation events. It is a wonderful way to celebrate your Recruit having earned the title of United States Marine. Thursday is Family Day and Friday is Graduation Day. The Marine Corps will have activities planned for both days.

There is no limit to the number of family members and friends that can attend Family Day or Graduation. You'll want to arrive at the Depot early to avoid long lines at the gate. Dress is casual. Please remember that this is an important time in your Marine's life and you do not want to put him in an uncomfortable position with his command and fellow Marines. Bare midriffs and suggestive attire are not appropriate. Comfortable walking shoes are suggested for both days. Wheelchairs and strollers are NOT available at MCRDSD;

however, the Depot is easily traversed by wheelchairs and motorized scooters.

Family Day includes the Drill Instructors Brief, the Motivational Run, Liberty Formation and Depot Liberty. The Drill Instructors Brief starts out your day. Here you'll learn what to do and what not to do during your time at MCRDSD. The drill instructors will then lead you to the Motivational Run. This is where you'll get your first glimpse of your new Marine! Following the Liberty Formation your new Marine will have Depot Liberty and be able to spend some time with you. You can have lunch together, relax, visit the Museum, shop, explore unrestricted parts of MCRDSD and, of course, take lots of photos!

Graduation Day includes the Color Ceremony and Graduation Ceremony. The Color

Ceremony is an optional event where you will see the raising of the flags and enjoy hearing the Marine Band. The Graduation Ceremony is the culmination of your new Marine's time at boot camp and the beginning of a new stage in his career.

Important Note: Due to some holiday schedules, a handful of recruit classes might graduate on a Wednesday, with family day on Tuesday. The same schedule will apply, just substitute Tuesday for Thursday and Wednesday for Friday in the schedule below. Changes in the levels of security alerts could alter scheduled events. Maps of the Depot and a schedule of events will be provided to you on Family Day.

Family Day: Thursday at MCRD

Plan to have breakfast and familiarize yourself with the Depot before the Drill Instructors Brief at 9:30 a.m.

Time	Event	Location	Description
6:30-9:00 a.m.	Breakfast Buffet	The Bay View Restaurant	An optional event. Your Marine will not be joining you for breakfast.
9:30 a.m.	Drill Instructors Brief	MCRD Command Museum	Family & friends learn the Do's and Don'ts for Family Day.

10:30 a.m.	Motivational Run	MCRD Command Museum	The "Moto Run" is your first opportunity to see your new Marine. They run in both directions; left to right then right to left. Pictures can best be taken if you remain in one spot.

12:00 p.m.	Liberty Formation	Shepherd Field Parade Deck	Drill Instructors will guide you to where you should sit. Please remember not to walk on the Parade Deck!
12:30-6:00 p.m.	Depot Liberty	Recruits must remain on the depot	The new Marines and their families have some time to relax

			and explore the Depot.
12:00-4:30 p.m.	Liberty Lunch Buffet	The Bay View Restaurant	An optional event. Enjoy a relaxing lunch and meet the Drill Instructors.
6:00 p.m.	Liberty Ends	Recruits must return to barracks.	

During Liberty, your Marine must remain on the Depot. Certain recruit training areas are off-limits to visitors. Recommended activities include having lunch and meeting the Drill Instructors at the Bay View Restaurant, visiting

Time	Event	Location	Description
6:30-9:00a.m.	Breakfast Buffet	Bay View Restaurant	An optional event. Your Marine will not be joining you for breakfast.
8:00-8:30 a.m.	Color Ceremony	Commanding General's Headquarters	Raising of the flags. Performances by the Marine Band and Color Guard.
8:45-9:30a.m.	Graduation Seating	Shepherd Field Parade Deck	You should be in your seats by 9:45 a.m.
10:00 a.m.-12:00 p.m.	Graduation Ceremony	Shepherd Field Parade Deck	A day every Marine will

			remember for life as one of his greatest achievements.
11:00 a.m.-1:30 p.m.	Friday Hot Lunch Buffet	Bay View Restaurant	An optional event. New Marines receive a free lunch with the minimum of one guest paid per Marine.

MCRD San Diego Command Museum, and shopping at the Marine Corps Exchange.

Graduation Day: Friday at MCRD

Plan to attend the color ceremony if possible. For graduation, the Depot schedule suggests arriving at the reviewing stands by 9:30 a.m.

and to be seated by 9:45 a.m. However, the stands will fill up earlier on Friday, so it's recommended that you obtain your seats by 8:45 a.m. if you want to be in the same or approximately the same seat you had on Thursday. After graduation, you may stay and visit the Depot, have lunch, and continue shopping.

Dining Services on the Depot

Mobile Snack Wagon

The Snack Wagon offers chips, candy, and drinks while you are attending the ceremonies. On Thursdays they are located outside the Depot Theater. On Fridays they are located behind the Reviewing Stand.

Family Day hours: 9:00 a.m. – 1:00 p.m.

Graduation Day hours: 8:30 a.m. – 11:00 a.m.

Starbucks Coffee

Located next to Building 10

Family Day and Graduation Day hours: 6:00 a.m. – 6:00 p.m.

Picnic People

Located at the Marine Corps Exchange Mall

A lunch menu is offered on Family Day from 12:00 p.m. – 4:30 p.m.

Subway Sandwiches

Available at the Marine Corps Exchange Mall on Graduation Day

Locker Room Bar & Grill

When you visit the recreation center, don't forget to stop at the Locker Room sports bar and grill located inside the Recreation Center. The Locker Room's menu includes California pizza, burgers & fries, buffalo wings, Swedish meatballs, and nachos.

Bar hours on Family Day and Graduation Day:

Thursday 1:00 p.m. – 11:00 p.m.

Friday 1:00 p.m. – 12:30 a.m.

Snack Bar hours Family Day and Graduation Day:

Thursday 11:00 a.m. – 5:00 p.m.

Friday 11:00 a.m. – 11:00 p.m.

The Bay View Restaurant

Free Depot Shuttle service is provided from the Depot Theater to the Bay View Restaurant. The Bay View offers an opportunity to relax in a beautiful water-front setting near San Diego Bay. There is a beautiful view of the water, palm trees, gardens and the MCRD Marina. Additional amenities include a bar, restrooms, and pay phones. Thursday's lunch offers outdoor dining as well as dining in the air-conditioned restaurant.

Family Day and Graduation Day hours:

Breakfast, Thursday 6:30 a.m. – 9:00 a.m.

Lunch, Thursday 12:00 p.m. – 4:30 p.m.

Breakfast, Friday 6:30 a.m. – 9:00 a.m.

Lunch, Friday 11:00 a.m. – 1:30 p.m.

Bayview Restaurant Menus, Prices & Schedule			
Thursday Family Day Breakfast Buffet	Thursday Liberty Lunch Buffet	Friday Graduation Day Breakfast Buffet	Friday Hot Buffet Lunch
6:30 a.m. – 9:00 a.m.	12:00 p.m. – 4:30 p.m.	6:30 a.m. – 9:00 a.m.	11:00 a.m. – 1:30 p.m.

$8.95 (Kids $4.95)	$13.95 (Kids $7.50)	$8.95 (Kids $4.95)	$9.50 (Kids $4.75)
Buffet-style. No sales tax. Includes gratuity. Indoor and outdoor seating. Major credit cards accepted.			
Menu Includes: fresh fruit, scrambled eggs, home fries, sausage links, apple pancakes,	**Menu Includes:** garden salad, baked chicken breast, hand-carved top round of beef,	**Menu Includes:** fresh fruit, scrambled eggs, breakfast potatoes, smoked ham, biscuits, sausage	Newly graduated Marines receive free Friday hot lunch buffet in the Bay View dining

assorted Danish pastries, mini muffins, donut holes, orange juice, coffee, and tea.	mashed potatoes and gravy, corn, rolls & butter, iced tea, coffee.	gravy, assorted Danish pastries, mini muffins, donut holes, orange juice, coffee, and tea.	room with minimum one paid guest per Marine.

Shopping Services on the Depot Marine Corps Exchange, Electronics, Home Store, Outdoor Store and the Cellar

You must be accompanied by your Marine. During graduation week the Exchange stores open at 8:00 a.m.

Marine Mart

You do not have to be accompanied by your Marine.

Drinks, sandwiches, and other convenience store items

Hours: Monday – Friday 6:00 a.m. – 10:00 p.m., Saturday/Sunday 7:00 a.m. – 7:00 p.m.

Marine Corps Store, located in the Marine Corps Exchange

You do not have to be accompanied by your Marine.

USMC gifts and merchandise

Hours: Thursday 7:30 a.m. – 5:00 p.m. and Friday until 4:00 p.m.

Recruit Sales Complex

You must be accompanied by your Marine.

Open for family members only on Thursday.

Basic items that Marines need during their Marine career.

Tickets & Tours

You must be accompanied by your Marine. Discounted tickets to Southern California attractions.

Places of Interest on the Depot

Recreation Center

Arcade games, pool tables, gaming center, bowling, free wi-fi, computer terminals, big screen TV's.

Hours on Family Day: 9:00 a.m. – 11:00 p.m.

Hours on Graduation Day: 9:00 a.m. – 12:30 a.m.

The Depot Command Museum

The museum includes a video theater, five permanent galleries, an art collection, a research center, and a gift shop.

Hours: Monday – Saturday 8:00 a.m. – 4:00 p.m.

Shuttle Schedule

Hotel Shuttles

Hotel shuttles only operate between your hotel and the Depot Theater. Drop-off and pick-up is in front of the Depot Theater. Check with your hotel for its shuttle schedule to and from MCRDSD.

MCRD Shuttles

MCRDSD provides free shuttle service on Family Day and Graduation Day. Every twenty minutes, beginning at 6:30 a.m., the shuttle buses travel around the Depot. The last shuttle leaves the Bay View Restaurant at 4:00 p.m. All shuttles begin at the Depot Theater.

The shuttle stops are:

Depot Theater

Depot Command Museum

Marine Corps Exchange

Bay View Restaurant

Motivational Run & Family Day

Motivational (MOTO) Run

Family Day begins with a motivational run referred to as the "MOTO Run." All graduating recruits run a 4-mile course which passes by all four training battalions, plus Support Battalion. At each battalion, selected recruits ring each of the Battalion Bells as the rest of the Company runs by singing cadence, loudly signaling successful completion of Recruit Training.

As recruits run to the cadence of their Drill Instructors, parents, family members and friends line the streets and cheer as they try to find the face of their loved one among the crowd of new Marines.

Family Day

The brand new Marines are given on-base liberty during the day so they can spend time with their families, introduce them to their fellow new Marines and drill instructors, show them the barracks, training areas, parade decks, and other areas where they trained, demonstrate proper liberty behavior, and most of all to share with their families their own personal stories about their transformation from civilian to Marine.

Press Release Template

Many Recruit Parents ask for a sample template they can use to send their local papers a press release upon their Recruit's graduation from boot camp. Below is a press release template for you to send to your local newspaper along with a photo of your new Marine.

FOR IMMEDIATE RELEASE

(Date)

(Your name)

(Your phone number)

PHOTO CAPTION

LOCAL MAN/WOMAN GRADUATES UNITED STATES MARINE CORPS BOOT CAMP

(Rank and Full Name), (Age), of (Name of Town) graduated from United States Marine Corps boot camp at Marine Corps Recruit Depot San Diego/Parris Island on Month XX, 20XX.

(Rank and Last Name) successfully completed 13 weeks of intensive basic training at MCRD San Diego/Parris Island as one of XX recruits in Training Platoon (number). While in recruit training (Rank and Last Name) accomplished/achieved the following: (add any accomplishments here, such as platoon leader, platoon artist, fire team leader). Following ten days home on leave he/she will report to Camp Pendleton/Camp Lejeune for (choose one: two months at Infantry Training Battalion or one month at Military Combat Training then Military Occupation Specialty school). (Rank, Last Name) will be stationed at (PDS) following training.

Section 5: What Happens After Boot Camp

Recruiter's Assistance after Boot Camp Graduation

While on leave, Marines may be selected by the USMC for participation in the Permissive Recruiter Assistance Support Program (PRASP). If selected for the program, ensure you bring with you all endorsements related to such program upon checking in to SOI. Unless approved by HQMC (MMEA-11/ELTA), Infantry-bound and Reserves Marines are NOT authorized PRASP. During RA, the new Marine will spend time in their home town assisting the Recruiters. The new Marine can expect to spend time with recruiters talking to young men and women around town, at the mall and even high schools. Your new Marine will speak with people about joining the Marine Corps and what to expect once they've decided to join. Your Marine will also assist with preparing poolees physically and mentally for success at recruit training.

10-Day Leave After Boot Camp Graduation

The next phase of training after boot camp is SOI, or School of Infantry. Your new Marine is entitled to one day of travel and ten days leave after recruit training. Your new Marine may report to SOI early in order to save leave if desired. Your Marine should listen, read, pay attention to, and ask questions about his/her orders <u>before</u> departing the Recruit Depot. Your

Marine will have a copy of his/her orders with them when they leave the Recruit Depot. Your Marine is required to check in no later than 1300 (that's 1:00 p.m.) on the date designated on his/her orders. Your Marine can find these by looking on the signed receiving endorsement on the bottom front paper of his/her orders. Marines are required to report directly to the school if they arrive early; they are NOT to get a hotel room in town. While on leave, non-infantry Marines may contact their recruiter for participation in the Permissive Recruiter Assistance Support Program (PRASP). If selected by the recruiter for the program, ensure you bring with you all endorsements related to such program upon checking in to SOI. Unless approved by HQMC

(MMEA-11/ELTA), Infantry-bound and Reserves Marines are NOT authorized PRASP.

PDS: Permanent Duty Stations

Marines are assigned to a PDS, or Permanent Duty Station when formal training (Boot camp, SOI, and MOS) is complete. Your Marine may be stationed at any number of permanent duty stations around the world, depending on his/her MOS, or Military Occupational Specialty (the job that your Marine will do in the Marine Corps).

Glossary of Terms

AH-1G, AH-IJ: The armed version of the UH-1 helicopter. The initial Marine AH-1s were Army G models modified only with Navy compatible radios, Marine green paint and a rotor brake for shipboard operations.

Later Marine models such as the AH-1J were specifically designed for Marine aviation requirements and were twin-engine.

AO: Arial Observer - usually assigned to fly in second seat for Aerial Observation - primarily assigned from infantry, artillery, or intelligence billets.

AO: Area of operations, similar in definition to TAOR discussed below.

ARVN: Army of the Republic of Viet Nam.

BDA: Bomb Damage Assessment - given to fixed wing pilot by airborne AO at end of air to ground support mission.

BDE: The abbreviation for a US Army brigade.

BLT: Battalion Landing Team, a US Marine infantry battalion specifically task organized and equipped to conduct amphibious or helicopter-borne landings from the sea.

CH-34A, CH-34 D: Powered by a single reciprocating engine, this helicopter was the workhorse during the early years of the Vietnam era. It was used to ferry troops, deliver supplies and for medevac operations. It was commonly referred to as the "dog".

CH-37C: Powered with twin reciprocating engines, this heavy helicopter operated on a limited basis in the early years of the war, mainly for the retrieval of downed aircraft.

CH-46A, CH-46D: A twin gas turbine powered medium helicopter that replaced the UH-34D for troop and cargo lift, medevac, and other assigned missions.

CH-53A, CH-53D: A twin gas turbine powered heavy helicopter that replaced the CH-37C for the retrieval of downed aircraft, as well as the movement of heavy and large items of equipment such as trucks and artillery. The CH-53D was the improved version with more powerful engines.

CHARLEY RIDGE: A prominent ridge of mountainous terrain approximately 20 miles southwest of Da Nang that afforded the Viet Cong, also known as "Charley," a route from Laos into the Da Nang area. It was the site of many Marine operations aimed at disrupting Charley's movement of men and supplies.

CHINOOK: The generic name or nickname of the US Army's CH-47 heavy helicopter.

CIDG: Civil Indigenous Defense Group, a paramilitary, militia-type unit made up of local Vietnamese who participated in the defense of their own village or hamlet.

CO: The Commanding Officer, or Commander of a specific unit.

CP: Command Post, the location from which the CO commanded his unit. This could range from an extensive permanent building complex to a hole in the ground.

D/CS: Deputy Chief of Staff. The staff officer responsible for a specific function such as D/CS AIR (Aviation) at Headquarters, US Marine Corps, responsible for all aviation matters.

DET: Abbreviation for detachment, usually a parent organization's smaller detached unit capable of self-sustained operations. For example, DET, HMH-463 would indicate a small number (4-6) of CH-53 helicopters operating independently of the parent unit, HMH-463.

DMZ: The Demilitarized Zone separating North and South Viet Nam that was established by the United Nations at the time French Indochina was partitioned into the two countries. It was generally ignored by both sides during the war.

EAGLE FLIGHT: (also PACIFIER, KINGFISHER, SPARROWHAWK) A package of aircraft, on either ground or airborne alert, designated to respond to emergency situations or targets of opportunity by either inserting ground units or attacking by fire or both. The group usually consisted of a command helicopter, troop lift helicopters and attack helicopters.

In some instances, fixed wing attack aircraft were also added to the package.

FAC: Forward Air Controller - usually a pilot assigned to a ground unit for air-to-ground liaison between aviation and ground units.

GUARD Channel: The universal radio channel monitored by all aircraft on which emergency transmissions and requests for assistance are made.

H&MS: Headquarters and Maintenance Squadron, a unit of a Marine Aircraft Group that performs both administrative functions and intermediate level aircraft maintenance. In some cases, an H&MS would operate small numbers of specialized aircraft, such as the CH-37C from 1965-1967.

HARDHAT: An acronym for the aircrew member's protective helmet.

Hill 55: (and others such as Hill 845 etc.) A means of identifying hill formations on the metric maps used in Viet Nam. The numbers indicating the height above sea level in meters of the highest point of that particular formation.

HMH: Marine Heavy Helicopter Squadron, the first H means helicopter; the M means Marine; the second H means heavy.

HML: Marine Light Helicopter Squadron, the first H means helicopter; the M means Marine; the L means light.

HMM: Marine Medium Helicopter Squadron, the first H means helicopter; the M means Marine; the M means medium. (NOTE) The three numbers following these letters usually identified the original parent Marine Aircraft Group and the sequence in which the squadron was first commissioned. HMM-161 was the first squadron commissioned in MAG-16. HML-367 was the seventh squadron commissioned in MAG-36. There were exceptions. HMH-463 was not the third squadron commissioned in MAG-46. MAG-46 did not exist in the active force structure. It was then and still is a Marine Reserve Aircraft Group. As a wartime expedient both HMH-462 and HMH-463 were commissioned in other aircraft groups and, when operational, were transferred to MAG-36 and MAG-16 respectively.

I CORPS: Viet Nam was divided into 4 geographical areas known as Corps in order to delineate responsibility for the military operations therein. From north to south they were I Corps, II Corps, III Corps and IV Corps. Early in the war, The US Marines were designated responsible for I Corps, which extended from the DMZ in the north and included the provinces of Quang Tri, Thua Thien, Quang Nam, Quang Tin and Quang Ngai Province in the south.

IFR: Instrument Flight Rules, a condition during which a pilot is flying in the clouds on instruments, and without reference to either the natural horizon or the ground.

KIA: Killed In Action.

LPD: Landing Platform Dock, a Navy amphibious ship, capable of supporting and operating a small number of helicopters for an extended period of time. Usually, 4 to 6 on board with 2 being operated simultaneously.

LPH: Landing Platform Helicopter, a Navy amphibious ship, capable of supporting and operating a squadron of helicopters for an extended period of time, and capable of transporting and off-loading a battalion of Marines at the same time.

LZ: Landing Zone, an unimproved site where helicopters landed in the performance of their assigned mission.

M-60: The standard light machine gun of US Marines in Viet Nam, in both ground and aviation units. In helicopter squadrons, M-60s were mounted in fixed forward firing positions on UH-1E gunships, and on flexible pintle mounts in the UH-1E side doors as well. They were also employed in the door or windows of transport helicopters (UH-34, CH-46, CH-53).

MAB: Marine Amphibious Brigade, a temporary headquarters superimposed over such amphibious units as a Regimental Landing Team and a Provisional Marine Aircraft Group. The MAB was identical in mission and structure to the Marine Expeditionary Brigade (MEB.)

MABS: Marine Airbase Squadron, the housekeeping unit of a MAG.

MACV: Military Assistance Command Viet Nam, the senior US headquarter charged with overall responsibility for conduct of the war.

MAG: Marine Aircraft Group, the unit immediately superior to aircraft squadrons, A helicopter MAG typically would have the following squadrons: 3 HMMs, I HML, I HMH, 1 H&MS, and I MABS attached.

MEB: Marine Expeditionary Brigade, identical to the MAB discussed above.

MEDEVAC: Medical evacuation, the term generally used to identify the mission of Marine helicopters involved in rescuing wounded, injured, and sick personnel.

MMAF: Marble Mountain Air Facility, the home of MAG-16 from August, 1965 until May, 1971, located east of the Da Nang Air Base, on the beach, between China Beach and the Marble Mountains.

MOS: Military Occupational Specialty - four digit code for a specific job type.

MSO: A US Navy wood-hulled mine sweeper.

MUV: Marine Unit Vietnam, the temporary identification of Marine helicopter squadrons operating from Da Nang Air Base in 1965 prior to the arrival in country of MAG-16.

NSA: Naval Support Activity, a US Navy organization responsible for various support functions in the Da Nang area, such as port facilities, fuel storage areas, and hospitals, i.e., the NSA Hospital.

NVA: North Vietnamese Army.

NW: Northwest

0-1, 0-IC: A light single engine observation aircraft used for forward air control, artillery spotting and general reconnaissance, from 1962 to 1969.

OV-IOA: A twin turboprop, twin boom observation aircraft that replaced the 0-1s in 1968. It had significantly greater performance and carried a larger payload.

POW: Prisoner of War.

PROVMAG: Provisional Marine Aircraft Group, a temporary group organized for a limited period of time to meet a specific tactical or operational need.

QEC: Quick Engine Change, an expedient procedure developed to quickly change the engine of a downed helicopter in the field.

RLT: Regimental Landing Team, a US Marine infantry regiment specifically task organized and equipped to conduct amphibious or helicopter-borne landings from the sea.

RPG: Rocket Propelled Grenade, an enemy grenade fired from a device utilizing a small rocket propellant charge, greatly increasing its normal range.

RVN: Republic of Viet Nam.

SAR: Search and Rescue, the mission assigned to either dedicated aviation units or other available aviation units related to locating and extracting downed aircrews and other personnel. The term CSAR identified Combat Search and Rescue units of the Air Force and Navy who were specifically trained and equipped to operate in heavily defended North Vietnamese airspace to conduct SAR missions.

SAR NORTH: The SAR mission north of the DMZ assigned in the early years of the war to Marine HMM squadrons, prior to the assignment of the specific CSAR units discussed above.

SHU-FLY: The name coined for the initial introduction of USMC helicopters into Viet Nam in 1962.

SLF: Special Landing Force, the designation of the USMC BLT and HMM squadron assigned to the Seventh Fleet Amphibious

Ready Group. The SLF regularly conducted amphibious operations across Vietnamese beaches into areas of suspected VC and NVA activity.

SW: Southwest.

TAC(A): Tactical Air Controller (Airborne) - either a qualified pilot or a qualified Aerial Observer who is responsible for the safe conduct of air-to-ground strikes, artillery strikes or naval gunfire missions.

TAOR: Tactical Area of Responsibility, the geographical area assigned to a military unit having responsibility for all operations therein, i.e., the First Marine Division's TAOR was the city of Da Nang and surrounding areas defined by specific features such as rivers, roads etc.

TF: Task Force, a unit temporarily organized to carry out a specific short term mission.

UH-1, UH-IB, UH-1E: The "Huey" was the standard US Army troop carrying helicopter in Viet Nam. The Marine version, the UH-1E was able to operate from shipboard. It performed command and control, liaison, observation, gunship, and medevac missions.

UH-34D: The standard USMC medium helicopter at the beginning of the war. It served in Viet Nam from April, 1962 until August, 1969.

UA: Unauthorized Absence, both a disciplinary term, and an acronym for anything or person not in the place it is expected to be.

UTT: Utility Tactical Transport, the name of the Army's UH-1B gunship unit early in the war when the helicopter gunship was still in an experimental state.

VC: Viet Cong, or Charley, the original enemy in South Viet Nam.

VMO: Marine Observation Squadron, the V means fixed wing; the M means Marine; the 0 means observation.

VNAF: Vietnamese Air Force.

WIA: Wounded in Action.

XO: Executive Officer, the second in command of a unit.

ZERO/ZERO: Zero ceiling, zero forward visibility, as in IFR flight conditions.

Glossary Part II (with a little slang thrown in)

ABOARD: on base; with us.

ACTUAL: radio talk for unit commander.

ALL HANDS: everyone.

AMTRACK: amphibious tractor; landing craft.

AO DAI (Viet.): formal attire worn by Vietnamese women.

AS YOU WERE: resume what you were doing; correction.

ASSHOLES AND ELBOWS: in a hurry; quickly.

BA MUI BA ("33"): Vietnamese beer.

BAC SI (Viet.): Doctor, used for Corpsman.

BAM: Broad Ass Marine; derogatory name for Woman Marine.

BARRACKS COVER: garrison (frame) cap.

BATTLE PIN: necktie clip.

BCD: Bad Conduct Discharge.

BELAY: stop; quit.

BILLET: assignment or job; place of residence.

BIRD: aircraft. BLOUSE: n. jacket; v. tuck in, secure.

BLOUSING BANDS: elastic bands used to secure utility trouser cuffs.

BLUES: Dress Blues.

BLT: Battalion Landing Team.

BOONDOCKS (BOONIES): rugged isolated back country.

BOONDOCKERS: low-topped work boots issued to reservists.

BOOT: recruit.

BOO-COO: (Fr. beaucoup) much, many.

BRAIN HOUSING GROUP: your gourd, mind, brain, or head.

BRASS: officers.

BRIG: jail.

BRIG RAT: jail inmate.

BRIG CHASER: MP assigned to escort prisoners.

BROTHER: black Marine (also Splib).

BROWN SIDE-OUT: desert camouflage pattern.

BULKHEAD: wall.

BY-THE-NUMBERS: in sequence.

CANNON COCKERS: artillerymen.

CARRY ON: resume what you were doing; as you were.

CASUAL COMPANY: unit of Marines awaiting reassignment.

CC: Corrective Custody; jail, the brig.

CHUCK: black Marine's term for white Marine.

CG: Commanding General.

CHIEU HOI (Viet.): freedom; safe conduct pass; program whereby VC who surrendered were assured safe conduct.

CHIMPO: see choda.

CHIT: written authorization or receipt.

CHODA: same as chimpo.

CHOW: food.

CHOW HALL: mess hall.

CLICK: one notch of adjustment on a rifle.

CINDERELLA LIBERTY: time off which ends at midnight.

CO (Viet.): girl, woman.

COLORS: n. the flag; v. ceremony of raising or lowering the flag.

CON BIET? (Viet) do you understand?

C-RATS: C rations, canned field rations.

COM RATS: commuted rations; in lieu pay for meals eaten off base.

CORPSMAN: Navy medic serving with Marines.

COVER: hat.

COVER ASS: take precautions to avoid blame.

THE CROTCH: derogatory term for Marine Corps.

CRUISE: period of enlistment; tour of duty.

DECK: floor.

DEUCE-AND-A-HALF: 2 1/2 ton truck.

DI-DI (Viet.): leave, go, move out.

DI-DI MAU (Viet.): emphatic of Di-di.

DIDDY BAG: cloth, drawstring bag for small items.

DIDDY BOP: swagger; affected walk.

DINK: Vietnamese.

DINKY-DAU (Viet): crazy.

DOG-AND-PONY-SHOW: special presentation put on for visiting dignitaries.

DOUBLE TIME: quickly; at a run.

DRY FIRE: practice.

DRY RUN: practice.

DU-DIT (Viet): fuck you!

EIGHTH & EYE: Headquarters Marine Corps.

ENTRENCHING TOOL (E-TOOL): small folding field shovel.

EVERY SWINGING DICK: All hands, everyone.

EYE FUCK: scrutinize; inspect closely.

FARTSACK: mattress cover.

FIELD DAY: general cleanup of barracks.

FIELD SCARF: necktie.

FIELD STRIP: disassemble; take apart.

FIRE IN THE HOLE: warning that explosives are about to be detonated.

FIRST SHIRT (ALSO TOP): First Sergeant.

FLOAT PHASE: sea deployment of a Marine unit.

FMF: Fleet Marine Force.

FOUR-BY: light truck.

FRONT LEANING REST POSITION: pushup position ("the Position").

GALLEY: kitchen.

GANG WAY: stand back! move away!

GEDUNK: sweets or a store that sells sweets.

GEAR: equipment.

GI CAN: garbage can.

GIZMO: gadget; anything that defies description.

GOURD: head; where you hang your cover.

GREEN SIDE-OUT: woodland pattern camouflage.

GRAB A HAT: leave.

GRINDER: parade ground.

GUIDON: pennant bearing unit designation.

GUNG HO: lit. work together; (from Chinese) highly motivated.

GUNGY: gung ho.

GUNNY: Gunnery Sergeant.

GRABASS (ORGANIZED GRABASS): play; sports, frivolous activity.

GREEN MACHINE: Marine Corps.

HAM: Hairy Assed Marine; male Marine.

HAM AND MOTHERS: "Ham and Motherfuckers;" generally detested C-ration meal posing as ham and lima beans.

HATCH: door.

HARD CHARGER: motivated Marine.

HEAD: toilet.

HIGH-AND-TIGHT: standard Marine haircut; shaved sides and short on top.

HOLLYWOOD MARINE: San Diego MCRD graduate.

HOOCH (Jap.): any kind of shelter, residence.

HONCHO (Jap.): boss; man in charge.

HOUSE MOUSE: Drill Instructor's go-fer.

HUMP: to march; to carry; to be burdened with.

HUSS: a favor; a break e.g., "gimme a huss;" archaic name for HU34D helicopter.

INCOMING: hostile fire being received!

IRISH PENNANT: string dangling from clothing indicating unkempt appearance.

ITR: Infantry Training Regiment.

JARHEAD: Marine.

JIBS: teeth, esp. front incisors, e.g., "I'll bust your jibs."

JING (also jing-wa, Jap.): change; money.

JOE SHIT THE RAGMAN: bad example, un-squared-away Marine, boyfriend of Rosy Rottencrotch.

JUNK-ON-THE-BUNK: complete clothing and equipment inspection (also Things-on-the-Springs) laid out on the rack.

K-BAR: Marine-issue fighting knife.

KLICK: kilometer.

LADDER (or ladderway): stairs.

LAI DAY (Viet.): come here!

LEAVE: authorized absence of more than 24 hours.

LIBERTY: authorized absence of less than 24 hours.

LOCK AND LOAD: arm and ready your weapon; get ready!

MAKE A HOLE: stand back! gang way!

MAGGIE'S DRAWERS: red disc used on the rifle range to signify missing the target.

MOS: assigned job specialty.

MUSTANG (Mustanger): enlisted man who becomes an officer.

NON-QUAL: Marine who fails to fire a qualifying score at the rifle range.

OFFICE HOURS: summary court marshall, official inquiry or reprimand.

OFFICE POGUE: desk-bound Marine.

ONTOS: armored tracked vehicle mounting six 106 mm recoilless rifles.

OUTSTANDING: exceptional; well done!

OVERHEAD: ceiling.

OVER THE HILL: absent without authorization.

OVER THE HUMP: more than halfway through enlistment.

PASSAGEWAY: corridor; hallway.

PIECE: rifle.

PISS CUTTER: envelope-shaped overseas cap.

PISS-AND-PUNK: bread and water punishment.

PISS TUBE: field urinal; rocket launcher (bazooka) which resembles one.

POGUE: lazy individual, also office worker.

POGEY BAIT: candy, sweets.

POLICE CALL: time allocated to clean up an area.

POLICE UP: clean up.

POOP (also dope, scoop): information.

POP-FLARE: hand held and launched aerial illumination flare.

PT: Physical Training; exercise.

QUARTERS: living space.

RACK: bed, bunk.

RAPPEL: descend from cliff or helicopter by rope.

RECON (also Force Recon): Force Reconnaissance Marine.

ROMP 'N' STOMP: to drill, march.

ROUND: bullet or artillery or mortar shell.

RUBBER LADY: inflatable air mattress.

SALT: experience; an old-timer Marine.

SALTY: smart-mouthed; opinionated.

SCOSHI (or scosh'): small, short, a little bit.

SCUTTLEBUTT: rumors; a drinking fountain.

SEABAG: duffle bag.

SEA DUTY: billeted aboard a ship.

SEA GOING BELLHOP: derog. for Marine, from Marines assigned to the bridge of a vessel.

SEA STORY: a lie or an exaggeration.

SEA LAWYER: self-appointed expert.

SECURE: tie down or make fast; also to recycle or dispose of; to put something in its proper place; to desist.

SEVEN-EIGHTY-TWO GEAR: field equipment; canvas web gear.

SHIT BIRD: messy or undisciplined; a fuck up.

SHIT CAN: (v) to dispose of; (n) garbage can.

SHORT: nearing the end of a tour of duty or enlistment.

SHORT ROUND: ordnance which is landing short of the intended target.

SHORT TIME: a very brief love affair.

SHORTTIMER: Marine nearing the end of an enlistment period.

SICK BAY: clinic or hospital.

SIX-BY (six-by-six): standard three-axle truck.

SIX-SIX-AND-A-KICK: The ultimate General court marshall punishment consisting of six months forfeiture of pay, six months hard labor, and a dishonorable discharge.

SKIPPER: captain; commanding officer.

SKIVVIES: underwear.

SKIVVIE HONCHO: a lothario; a ladies man.

SKIVVIE HOUSE: brothel.

SLOPCHUTE: diner; restaurant.

SMOKING LAMP: authority to smoke when it is lit.

SNAP IN: practice, esp. on the rifle range.

SNOOPIN' AND POOPIN': reconnoitering.

SNOT LOCKER: nose.

SOUND OFF: assertively voice.

SORRY 'BOUT THAT: assertion of mock apology.

SPUD LOCKER: pantry.

SQUAD BAY: barracks.

SQUARED AWAY: neat, orderly, organized.

SQUID: (derog.) sailor.

STACK ARMS: command given to place 3 rifles in a pyramid.

STACKING SWIVEL: appendage near muzzle of rifle allowing stacked arms; neck.

STAND BY: prepare.

STANDBY: waiting status.

STARCHIES: starched utilities.

STROKE BOOK: porno magazine.

SURVEY: dispose of; recycle.

SWAB: mop.

SWABBIE: sailor.

TI TI (Viet.) (pron. tee-tee): little, small.

TOP: Sergeant Major.

TOPSIDE: upstairs; on deck.

TROPS: khaki tropical summer dress uniform.

TURN TO: begin work.

UA: Unauthorized Absence.

UD: Undesirable Discharge.

UTILITIES: olive drab field uniform.

WILLIE PETER: white phosphorus.

THE WORD: confirmed official information; the straight scoop.

ZERO-DARK-THIRTY: pre-dawn; early.

Resources

Here follows a list of Marine Corps resources:

Website: www.marines.mil

Blog: marines.dodlive.mil

Magazine: marinesmagazine.dodlive.mil

Broadcast: www.marines.mil/MarinesTV

Facebook: facebook.com/marines

YouTube: www.youtube.com/marines

Twitter: www.twitter.com/USMC

Flickr: www.flickr.com/marine_corps

Social media inbox: Marines@dma.mil

Additionally, here are couple of sites that help you connect to the Marine Corps community:

emarine.org

recruitparents.com

American Red Cross

Emergency contact assistance

http://www.redcross.org

Blue Star Mothers

Non-partisan and non-political organization of military mothers

http://www.bluestarmothers.org

http://www.fortwayneareabluestarmothers.com

Boot Camp Graduation (non-USMC site)

Max Beerup is very informative, knowledgeable and helpful!

http://www.usmcgradsandiego.org

Boot Camp Graduation (non-USMC site)

By Gretchen Miller

http://www.usmcgradparrisisland.org

Camp Lejeune , NC (Pronounced "Luh-Jern" – not "Le-June")

MCT/SOI Training after Boot Camp, MOS and Fleet

http://www.lejeune.usmc.mil

Camp Pendleton, CA

MCT/SOI Training after Boot Camp, MOS and Fleet

http://www.ccp.usmc.mil

Marine Corps Recruiting Depot (MCRD) Parris Island, SC

Boot Camp

http://www.mcrdpi.usmc.mil

Marine Corps Recruiting Depot (MCRD) San Diego, CA

Boot Camp

http://www.mcrdsd.usmc.mil

Marine Toys for Tots Foundation

Fort Wayne has local organization operated by Marine Reserves

http://www.ft-wayne-in.toysfortots.org

Marine Wives

A great resource for spouses of Marines

http://www.marinewives.com

MCRD San Diego Recruit Grad Gear

Allow 3-4 weeks for order delivery

http://www.mccsmcrd.com

National Museum of the Marine Corps

Quantico, VA

http://www.usmcmuseum.org

Operation Care Package

Not-for-Profit organization supporting our

deployed heros

http://www.operationcarepackages.org

Ship It APO

Layperson's guide to overseas deployed military

mail and shipments

http://www.shipitapo.com

United States Marine Corps

Official USMC Web Site with a Parents Section

http://www.usmc.mil

U. S. Marine Corps Gear

Official Marine Corps Clothing and Products

http://www.grunt.com

USO

Official Military Service Organization with locations at major airports

http://www.uso.org

References

Marine Parents - www.recruitparents.com

eMarine.org

www.usmc.mil

USMC History Division -

https://www.mcu.usmc.mil/historydivision/SitePages/Home.aspx

Recruit Depot Parris Island -

http://www.mcrdpi.marines.mil/

Parris Island Museum -

http://www.parrisislandmuseum.com/

Author Bio

A.J. Cabrera is an author and freelance writer. She has written for several national and trade publications covering such topics as parenting, martial arts, the military and more. As a United States Marine Corps veteran, her experiences there helped to shape her life perceptions about the world around her, as well as define her personal relationships with others. She continues to acquire a personal understanding of cultural issues to further her education, thereby increasing her effectiveness as a versatile freelance writer, author, researcher and human being. On her spare time, she enjoys continuing her education on a variety of subjects. It is her faith in God and loyal convictions to her core values that enable her success.

More Books by A. J. Cabrera

Marine Corps Boot Camp Survival Guide: How to Prepare for (And Live Through) Marine Corps Boot Camp

The Parent's Guide to Surviving Marine Corps Boot Camp

Empowering Writing Prompts That Will Change Your Life (If You Let Them)

Hot Story Ideas for Fiction Writers

The Fleshy Fat Suit

The Journal Art Shop: 36 Art Journaling Background Methods, Techniques and Ideas

Thank You Page

Before you go, I would just like to say "thank you" for purchasing my book. There are many books out there but you took a chance on mine. So, a big thank you for downloading this book and reading it all the way to the end.

If you liked what you have read, then please leave a review on Amazon. This feedback will help me continue to write the kind of Kindle books that help you get results.

www.ingramcontent.com/pod-product-compliance
Lightning Source LLC
Chambersburg PA
CBHW051629170526
45167CB00001B/113